Collector's Library

AS YOU LIKE IT

AS YOU LIKE IT

William Shakespeare

INTRODUCTION BY
NED HALLEY

Collector's Library

This edition published in 2012 by
Collector's Library
an imprint of CRW Publishing Limited,
69 Gloucester Crescent, London NW1 7EG

ISBN 978 1 907360 60 2

2 4 6 8 10 9 7 5 3 1

Typeset in Great Britain by
Bookcraft Ltd, Stroud, Gloucestershire

Printed and bound in China by Imago

Contents

INTRODUCTION

As You Like It lays on the theme of love with the proverbial trowel. A drama dedicated to the eternal comedy of the human condition, built around a famously whimsical plot, it is among the best-loved and most regularly staged masterpieces of the Shakespeare canon. It is certainly one of the most entertaining of the plays, resounding with newly minted idioms from the very 'laid on with a trowel' that chides the jester Touchstone for his grandiloquence in Act I Scene II to Rosalind's plea that it is not 'too much of a good thing' to wish for a prompt and perfect marriage, to Orlando, in Act IV Scene II.

Delightful though stagings, screenings and broadcasts might be, a play as bejewelled as this can lose much in the translation. Shakespeare, Samuel Johnson was brave enough to say, is all too often ruined in the performance. *As You Like It* in particular is a play that repays reading, because it is among the most extraordinary studies of human nature in all literature. As Dr Johnson tells us, Shakespeare is 'the poet of nature; the poet that holds up to his readers a faithful mirror of manners and of life'. And in this play, Johnson's immortal observation is vividly manifested: 'In the writings of other poets a character is too often an individual; in those of Shakespeare it is commonly a species.'

Believed to have been completed between 1599 and 1600, the Bard's most prolific patch (the same period also yielded up *Hamlet*, *Julius Caesar* and *Twelfth Night*), the play was registered by name for copyright at the Stationers' Company in London on 4 August 1600, but there is no quarto edition (a booklet of four-page sections made from twice-folded paper sheets) of the kind in which many of the other plays first appeared. In fact there is no extant edition before the printing of the collected works, the *First Folio*, published in 1623, seven years after Shakespeare's death.

The early life of the play is made the more mysterious by lack of evidence it was ever performed in the author's lifetime. There is no mention in the annals of the Lord Chamberlain's Men, the company of players with whom Shakespeare himself acted. No performance is recorded at Court (many of the plays were staged at the royal palace of Whitehall), or listed by the London theatres. Just one tantalising memory beckons. It is the belief among the Herbert family, earls of Pembroke, of Wilton House in Wiltshire that on 2 December 1603, *As You Like It* was performed there. The third Earl, a patron of the Chamberlain's Men and later a sponsor of the *First Folio*, had laid on the entertainment for his guest, King James I, who with his court stayed at the palatial Herbert home near Salisbury during an outbreak of plague in London. The Lord Chamberlain's Men, renamed the King's Men in honour of James's succession on the death of Queen Elizabeth I earlier that year, reputedly gave the performance, for a princely fee of £30. There is a story, too, that Lord Pembroke's mother, Mary, sister of Sir Philip Sidney and a literary figure in her own right, invited Shakespeare to the Wilton performance, where he took the role of Adam, servant to Orlando's family.

While none of these intriguing possibilities have been substantiated by scholars there are no such doubts about the literary provenance of the play. Shakespeare took the story from *Rosalynde*, a popular prose romance (what we would now call a novel) by the adventurer and writer Thomas Lodge, published in 1590. The setting, the Ardennes in France, along with the complete narrative of the usurped duchy and the exile of characters including eponymous heroine Rosalind to a forest are all lifted from Lodge's tale, which in its turn was partly inspired by the medieval verse *The Tale of Gamelyn*, a story with strong parallels to the legend of the dispossessed nobleman turned outlaw Robin Hood.

Shakespeare adapts Lodge's Ardennes to the sylvan idyll of the Forest of Arden – perhaps a portmanteau word for paradise from Arcadia and Eden – but he maintains a Continental mood with French names for characters such as Amiens, Le Beau and Jaques and occasional deliberate allusions to the host state (Orlando is the 'stubbornest young fellow of France', declares his brother Oliver). It was a necessary precaution when portraying the antics of the ruling class to cast the characters as foreign (Italian, usually) to obviate any comparison with figures from the English Court which was, after all, the principal patron of the drama of Shakespeare's time.

But location is incidental in this play. The forest is metaphor, a bucolic counterpoint to the vainglory of the court of the usurper duke Frederick, who has stolen his brother's birthright, and cast the Duke Senior (as his elder is curiously identified among the Dramatis Personae) out of his former dominions to the

> Forest of Arden, and a many many men with him; and there they live like the old
> Robin Hood of England; they say many young gentlemen flock to him every
> day, and fleet the time carelessly, as they did in the golden world.

This is the account given in the first scene of the play by the wrestler 'Monsieur' Charles, who is supposed to be in the service of Duke Senior. The court, we soon learn, is a dark place of usurpation and greed, where the breaking of limbs in violent wrestling bouts counts as entertainment and courtiers connive at the maiming of their close relatives. As Oliver warns Charles in advance of his bout with Orlando, his younger brother, the wrestler would be better to break his neck than his finger, because:

> if thou dost him any slight disgrace, or if he do not mightily grace himself on thee,
> he will practise against thee by poison, entrap thee by some treacherous device, and

never leave thee till he hath ta'en thy life by some indirect means or other; for, I
assure thee, and almost with tears as I speak it, there is
not one so young and so
villainous this day living.

The lines drawn between good and evil in this play are very plain indeed. Even Oliver's cruel traducing of Orlando is outdone by the usurping duke Frederick, who exhibits that most odious of faults, bad sportsmanship, when his champion Charles is unexpectedly defeated by the young challenger in the wrestling match. Learning that the victor is the son of an old enemy, the late Roger de Bois, Frederick grudgingly acknowledges Orlando's skill, but qualifies it with:

Thou shouldst have better pleased me with this deed
Hadst thou descended from another house

Frederick's fury and resentment is soon manifested, when courtier Le Beau comes to give Orlando a diplomatic warning that 'such is now the duke's condition,/ That he misconstrues all that you have done'. Orlando is advised to make himself scarce. And in the best traditions of tyrant paranoia, Frederick now also turns on Rosalind because she too is the child of an enemy, none other than Duke Senior. Even though she has been tolerated at court since the banishment because she is inseparable from her cousin Celia, Frederick's sole heir, she is now told to go.

Within these ten days if that thou be'st found
So near our public court as twenty miles,
Thou diest for it.

Celia, outraged by this injustice, resolves to escape the court with Rosalind and head for the forest, Celia disguised in 'poor and mean attire' and Rosalind, 'because I am more than common tall,' as a man named Ganymede. They take with them an unlikely protector, the court jester Touchstone. Meanwhile Orlando, who will travel with Adam, his late father's servant (sacked by wicked Oliver for insubordination), will shortly follow. Orlando and Rosalind have already momentarily met at the scene of the wrestling match and, naturally, have fallen in love at first sight.

And so to Act II and their destination, the Forest of Arden. Duke Senior opens Scene I by welcoming his own informal court, mostly noblemen dressed as 'Foresters' to a setting that contrasts pointedly with that of his brother.

> Now, my co-mates and brothers in exile
> Hath not old custom made this life more sweet
> Than that of painted pomp? Are not these woods
> More free from peril than the envious court?

In this haven from the material machinations of his former domain, the Duke is enjoying a sequestered lifestyle he seems sincerely to prefer to his previous way of life. It is hardly a new concept, of course, being in the timeless tradition of finding refuge in the countryside from the rat race in town, a notion beloved of poets and dramatists from the ancient Greeks onwards. And in *As You Like It*, Shakespeare certainly warms to his theme. 'It is the most ideal of this author's plays,' wrote the essayist William Hazlitt in 1817. 'It is a pastoral drama in which the interest arises more out of the sentiments and characters than out of the actions or situations. It is not what is done, but what is said, that claims our attention. Nursed in solitude, "under the shade of melancholy boughs", the imagination grows soft and delicate, and the wit runs riot in idleness, like a spoiled child that is never sent to school. Caprices and fancy reign and revel here, and stern necessity is banished to the court.'

Here is Shakespeare cast as the romantic poet, which of course is exactly what he was. Filled with songs – *As You Like It* has the most of all the plays – the character of Rosalind, once she is abroad in the forest, is a masterful creation, both as individual and species. She balances good humour with instinctive compassion, and there is a quality of breathlessness in her speaking that wonderfully betrays the intensity of her feelings as she spars with Orlando. Her genuine love and feigned cynicism are exquisitely counterpointed in her riposte to her lover's vow that he will love her 'For ever and a day':

> Say a day without the ever: no, no, Orlando, men are
>   April when they woo, December
> when they wed: maids are May when they are maids,
>   but the sky changes when they are
> wives: I will be more jealous of thee than a Barbary
>   cock-pigeon over his hen; more
> clamorous than a parrot against rain; more newfan-
>   gled than an ape; more giddy in my
> desires than a monkey; I will weep for nothing, like
>   Diana in the fountain, and I will do
> that when you are disposed to be merry; I will laugh
>   like a hyen, and that when you are
> inclined to sleep.

If Rosalind's disguise as a young man seems an oddly contrived device, it is nevertheless one on which the playwright capitalises to great effect. The arch, piquant exchanges between Orlando and 'Ganymede' incorporate many telling observations on love and what lovers might say to each other if only they were not prevented from so doing by the circumstances or simple inhibitions that tongue-tie us all.

This sort of articulation extends to other characters in the play, and to great comic effect. Take Touchstone's confrontation with William, his rival for the hand of Audrey. While too many of us might sulk and mutter in such a stand-off, the jester takes the direct approach:

> abandon the society of this female; or, clown, thou
>   perishest; or, to thy better
> understanding, diest; or, to wit, I kill thee, make thee
>   away, translate thy life into death,

thy liberty into bondage. I will deal in poison with
thee, or in bastinado, or in steel; I
will bandy with thee in faction; will o'er-run thee with
policy; I will kill thee a hundred
and fifty ways; therefore tremble and depart.

Touchstone is an important balancing factor in this play.
While romance blossoms poetically elsewhere in the forest, he
is rather less lyrical about the prospects of betrothal to Audrey.
He tells the duke: 'I press in here, sir, amongst the rest of the
country copulatives, to swear and to forswear, according as
marriage binds and blood breaks. A poor virgin, sir, an ill-
favour'd thing, sir, but mine own'. And while the duke and all
around him seem content to subscribe to the pastoral dream of
'tongues in trees, books in the running brooks,/ Sermons in
stones, and good in everything' the jester takes a more prag-
matic view. When asked by the shepherd Corin for his own
opinion of the shepherd's life, Touchstone replies:

Truly, shepherd, in respect of itself, it is a good life;
but in respect that it is a
shepherd's life, it is naught. In respect that it is solitary, I like it very well; but in
respect that it is private, it is a very vile life. Now in
respect it is in the fields, it
pleaseth me well; but in respect it is not in the court, it
is tedious. As it is a spare
life, look you, it fits my humour; but as there is no
more plenty in it, it goes much
against my stomach.

And from Corin, Touchstone elicits this thoroughly real-
istic insight into his own philosophy:

I know the more one sickens the worse at ease he is;
and that he that wants
money, means, and content, is without three good
friends.

Touchstone and Jaques are the only two among the principal characters of *As You Like It* invented by Shakespeare. All others derive directly from the play's source, the romance *Rosalynde*. And while Touchstone contributes balance, Jaques, always the melancholy, adds a distinctly philosophical note to the play. He is, according to Hazlitt, 'the only purely contemplative character in Shakespeare' and it is into his mouth that the author puts the immortal words (in Act II Scene VII) for which this play is most celebrated:

> All the world's a stage,
> And all the men and women merely players;
> They have their exits and their entrances;
> And one man in his time plays many parts,
> His acts being seven ages.

It is Jaques too who gives the extraordinary report, earlier in the scene, about the motley fool he says he has met in the forest. The fool, he reports, consults a pocket watch – in Shakespeare's time a luxury novelty of vanishing rarity – and moralises on the topic of time.

> And then he drew a dial from his poke,
> And, looking on it with lack-lustre eye,
> Says very wisely, *It is ten o'clock;*
> *Thus we may see,* quoth he, *how the world wags;*
> *'Tis but an hour ago since it was nine;*
> *And after one hour more 'will be eleven;*
> *And so, from hour to hour, we ripe and ripe,*
> *And then, from hour to hour, we rot and rot;*
> *And thereby hangs a tale.*

ROSALIND Well, this is the Forest of Arden.

AS YOU LIKE IT

DRAMATIS PERSONAE

DUKE, *living in banishment.*
FREDERICK, *his brother, and usurper of his dominions.*
AMIENS, ⎫
JAQUES, ⎭ *lords attending on the banish'd Duke.*
LE BEAU, *a courtier attending on Frederick.*
CHARLES, *wrestler to Frederick.*
OLIVER, ⎫
JAQUES, ⎬ *Rowland de Boys.*
ORLANDO, ⎭
ADAM, ⎫
DENIS, ⎭ *servants to Oliver.*
TOUCHSTONE, *a clown.*
SIR OLIVER MARTEXT, *a vicar.*
CORIN, ⎫
SILVIUS, ⎭ *shepherds.*
WILLIAM, *a country fellow, in love with Audrey.*
A person representing HYMEN.

ROSALIND, *daughter to the banish'd Duke.*
CELIA, *daughter to Frederick.*
PHEBE, *a shepherdess.*
AUDREY, *a country wench.*

LORDS, PAGES, *and* ATTENDANTS, *etc.*

SCENE — *Oliver's house; Duke Frederick's court; and the Forest of Arden.*

OLIVER Wilt thou lay hands on me, villain?

ACT I

SCENE I

Orchard of OLIVER'S *house.*
Enter ORLANDO *and* ADAM.

ORLANDO
As I remember, Adam, it was upon this fashion: a'
bequeath'd me by will but poor a thousand crowns, and,
as thou say'st, charged my brother, on his blessing, to
breed me well: and there begins my sadness. My brother
Jaques he keeps at school, and report speaks goldenly of
his profit; for my part, he keeps me rustically at home, or,
to speak more properly, stays me here at home unkept;
for call you that keeping for a gentleman of my birth, that

differs not from the stalling of an ox? His horses are bred better; for, besides that they are fair with their feeding, they are taught their manage, and to that end riders dearly hired: but I, his brother, gain nothing under him but growth; for the which his animals on his dunghills are as much bound to him as I. Besides this nothing that he so plentifully gives me, the something that nature gave me his countenance seems to take from me: he lets me feed with his hinds, bars me the place of a brother, and, as much as in him lies, mines my gentility with my education. This is it, Adam, that grieves me; and the spirit of my father, which I think is within me, begins to mutiny against this servitude: I will no longer endure it, though yet I know no wise remedy how to avoid it.

ADAM
  Yonder comes my master, your brother.

ORLANDO
  Go apart, Adam, and thou shalt hear how he will shake me up.

Enter OLIVER.

OLIVER
  Now, sir! what make you here?

ORLANDO
  Nothing: I am not taught to make anything.

OLIVER
  What mar you then, sir?

ORLANDO
  Marry, sir, I am helping you to mar that which God made, a poor unworthy brother of yours, with idleness.

OLIVER
  Marry, sir, be better employ'd, and be naught awhile.

ORLANDO
  Shall I keep your hogs, and eat husks with them? What prodigal's portion have I spent that I should come to such penury?

OLIVER
  Know you where you are, sir?

ORLANDO

O, sir, very well: here in your orchard.

OLIVER

Know you before whom, sir?

ORLANDO

Ay, better than him I am before knows me. I know you are my eldest brother; and, in the gentle condition of blood, you should so know me. The courtesy of nations allows you my better, in that you are the first-born; but the same tradition takes not away my blood, were there twenty brothers betwixt us: I have as much of my father in me as you; albeit, I confess, your coming before me is nearer to his reverence.

OLIVER

What, boy!

ORLANDO

Come, come, elder brother, you are too young in this.

OLIVER

Wilt thou lay hands on me, villain?

ORLANDO

I am no villain; I am the youngest son of Sir Rowland de Boys; he was my father, and he is thrice a villain that says such a father begot villains. Wert thou not my brother, I would not take this hand from thy throat till this other had pull'd out thy tongue for saying so; thou hast rail'd on thyself.

ADAM

Sweet masters, be patient: for your father's remembrance, be at accord.

OLIVER

Let me go, I say.

ORLANDO

I will not, till I please: you shall hear me. My father charged you in his will to give me good education: you have train'd me like a peasant, obscuring and hiding from me all gentleman-like qualities. The spirit of my father grows strong in me, and I will no longer endure it:

therefore allow me such exercises as may become a gentleman, or give me the poor allottery my father left me by testament; with that I will go buy my fortunes.

OLIVER
And what wilt thou do? beg, when that is spent? Well, sir, get you in: I will not long be troubled with you; you shall have some part of your will: I pray you, leave me.

ORLANDO
I will no further offend you than becomes me for my good.

OLIVER
Get you with him, you old dog.

ADAM
Is 'old dog' my reward? Most true, I have lost my teeth in your service. — God be with my old master! he would not have spoke such a word.

[*Exeunt* ORLANDO *and* ADAM.

OLIVER
Is it even so? begin you to grow upon me? I will physic your rankness, and yet give no thousand crowns neither. — Holla, Denis!

Enter DENIS.

DENIS
Calls your worship?

OLIVER
Was not Charles, the duke's wrestler, here to speak with me?

DENIS
So please you, he is here at the door, and importunes access to you.

OLIVER
Call him in. [*Exit* DENIS.] 'Twill be a good way; and to-morrow the wrestling is.

Enter CHARLES.

CHARLES
Good morrow to your worship.

5

OLIVER

Good morrow, Monsieur Charles. — What's the new
news at the new court?

CHARLES

There's no news at the court, sir, but the old news: that
is, the old duke is banish'd by his younger brother the
new duke; and three or four loving lords have put
themselves into voluntary exile with him, whose lands
and revenues enrich the new duke; therefore he gives
them good leave to wander.

OLIVER

Can you tell if Rosalind, the duke's daughter, be
banish'd with her father?

CHARLES

O, no; for the duke's daughter, her cousin, so loves her,
being ever from their cradles bred together, that she
would have follow'd her exile, or have died to stay
behind her. She is at the court, and no less beloved of
her uncle than his own daughter; and never two ladies
loved as they do.

OLIVER

Where will the old duke live?

CHARLES

They say he is already in the forest of Arden, and a
many merry men with him; and there they live like the
old Robin Hood of England: they say many young
gentlemen flock to him every day, and fleet the time
carelessly, as they did in the golden world.

OLIVER

What, you wrestle to-morrow before the new duke?

CHARLES

Marry, do I, sir; and I came to acquaint you with a
matter. I am given, sir, secretly to understand that your
younger brother Orlando hath a disposition to come in
disguised against me to try a fall. To-morrow, sir, I
wrestle for my credit; and he that escapes me without
some broken limb shall acquit him well. Your brother is

but young and tender; and, for your love, I would be loath to foil him, as I must, for my own honour, if he come in: therefore, out of my love to you, I came hither to acquaint you withal, that either you might stay him from his intendment or brook such disgrace well as he shall run into, in that it is a thing of his own search and altogether against my will.

OLIVER

Charles, I thank thee for thy love to me, which thou shalt find I will most kindly requite. I had myself notice of my brother's purpose herein, and have by underhand means labour'd to dissuade him from it; but he is resolute. I'll tell thee, Charles: it is the stubbornest young fellow of France; full of ambition, an envious emulator of every man's good parts, a secret and villainous contriver against me his natural brother; therefore use thy discretion; I had as lief thou didst break his neck as his finger. And thou wert best look to't; for if thou dost him any slight disgrace, or if he do not mightily grace himself on thee, he will practise against thee by poison, entrap thee by some treacherous device, and never leave thee till he hath ta'en thy life by some indirect means or other; for, I assure thee, and almost with tears I speak it, there is not one so young and so villainous this day living. I speak but brotherly of him; but should I anatomise him to thee as he is, I must blush and weep, and thou must look pale and wonder.

CHARLES

I am heartily glad I came hither to you. If he come to-morrow, I'll give him his payment: if ever he go alone again, I'll never wrestle for prize more: and so, God keep your worship!

OLIVER

Farewell, good Charles. [Exit CHARLES.] Now will I stir this gamester: I hope I shall see an end of him; for my soul, yet I know not why, hates nothing more than he. Yet he's gentle; never school'd, and yet learned; full of noble device; of all sorts enchantingly beloved; and, indeed, so much in the heart of the world, and especially of my own people, who best know him, that I am altogether misprised: but it shall not be so long; this wrestler shall clear all: nothing remains but that I kindle the boy thither; which now I'll go about. [*Exit.*

SCENE II

Lawn before the DUKE'S *palace.*

Enter ROSALIND *and* CELIA.

CELIA

I pray thee, Rosalind, sweet my coz, be merry.

ROSALIND

Dear Celia, I show more mirth than I am mistress of; and would you yet I were merrier? Unless you could teach me to forget a banish'd father, you must not learn me how to remember any extraordinary pleasure.

CELIA

Herein I see thou lovest me not with the full weight that I love thee. If my uncle, thy banish'd father, had banish'd thy uncle, the duke my father, so thou hadst been still with me, I could have taught my love to take thy father for mine: so wouldst thou, if the truth of thy love to me were so righteously temper'd as mine is to thee.

ROSALIND

Well, I will forget the condition of my estate, to rejoice in yours.

CELIA

You know my father hath no child but I, nor none is like to have: and, truly, when he dies, thou shalt be his heir; for what he hath taken away from thy father perforce, I will render thee again in affection; by mine honour, I will; and when I break that oath, let me turn monster: therefore, my sweet Rose, my dear Rose, be merry.

ROSALIND
  From henceforth I will, coz, and devise sports.
  Let me see: what think you of falling in love?
CELIA
  Marry, I prithee, do, to make sport withal: but love no
  man in good earnest; nor no further in sport neither
  than with safety of a pure blush thou mayst in honour
  come off again.

ROSALIND What think you of falling in love?

ROSALIND

What shall be our sport, then?

CELIA

Let us sit and mock the good housewife Fortune from
her wheel, that her gifts may henceforth be bestow'd
equally.

ROSALIND

I would we could do so; for her benefits are mightily
misplaced; and the bountiful blind woman doth most
mistake in her gifts to women.

CELIA

'Tis true; for those that she makes fair, she scarce makes
honest; and those that she makes honest, she makes very
ill-favour'dly.

ROSALIND

Nay, now thou goest from Fortune's office to Nature's:
Fortune reigns in gifts of the world, not in the
lineaments of Nature.

Enter TOUCHSTONE.

CELIA

No? when Nature hath made a fair creature, may she
not by Fortune fall into the fire? Though Nature hath
given us wit to flout at Fortune, hath not Fortune sent
in this fool to cut off the argument?

ROSALIND

Indeed, there is Fortune too hard for Nature, when
Fortune makes Nature's natural the cutter-off of
Nature's wit.

CELIA

Peradventure this is not Fortune's work neither, but
Nature's; who perceiveth our natural wits too dull to
reason of such goddesses and hath sent this natural for
our whetstone; for always the dullness of the fool is the
whetstone of the wits. — How now, wit! whither wander
you?

TOUCHSTONE

Mistress, you must come away to your father.

CELIA

Were you made the messenger?

TOUCHSTONE

No, by mine honour; but I was bid to come for you.

ROSALIND

Where learn'd you that oath, fool?

TOUCHSTONE

Of a certain knight that swore by his honour they were good pancakes, and swore by his honour the mustard was naught: now I'll stand to it, the pancakes were naught, and the mustard was good; and yet was not the knight forsworn.

CELIA

How prove you that, in the great heap of your knowledge?

ROSALIND

Ay, marry, now unmuzzle your wisdom.

TOUCHSTONE

Stand you both forth now: stroke your chins, and swear by your beards that I am a knave.

CELIA

By our beards, if we had them, thou art.

TOUCHSTONE

By my knavery, if I had it, then I were; but if you swear by that that is not, you are not forsworn: no more was this knight, swearing by his honour, for he never had any; or if he had, he had sworn it away before ever he saw those pancakes or that mustard.

CELIA

Prithee, who is't that thou mean'st?

TOUCHSTONE

One that old Frederick, your father, loves.

CELIA

My father's love is enough to honour him enough: speak no more of him; you'll be whipp'd for taxation one of these days.

TOUCHSTONE
  The more pity, that fools may not speak wisely what wise men do foolishly.

CELIA
  By my troth, thou sayest true; for since the little wit that fools have was silenced, the little foolery that wise men have makes a great show. — Here comes Monsieur Le Beau.

ROSALIND
  With his mouth full of news.

CELIA
  Which he will put on us, as pigeons feed their young.

ROSALIND
  Then shall we be news-cramm'd.

CELIA
  All the better; we shall be the more marketable.

Enter LE BEAU.

  Bon jour, Monsieur Le Beau: what's the news?

LE BEAU
  Fair princess, you have lost much good sport.

CELIA
  Sport! of what colour!

LE BEAU
  What colour, madam! how shall I answer you?

ROSALIND
  As wit and fortune will.

TOUCHSTONE
  Or as the Destinies decrees.

CELIA
  Well said: that was laid on with a trowel.

TOUCHSTONE
  Nay, if I keep not my rank, —

ROSALIND
  Thou losest thy old smell.

LE BEAU
  You amaze me, ladies: I would have told you of good wrestling, which you have lost the sight of.

ROSALIND

Yet tell us the manner of the wrestling.

LE BEAU

I will tell you the beginning; and, if it please your
ladyships, you may see the end; for the best is yet to do;
and here, where you are, they are coming to perform it.

CELIA

Well, — the beginning, that is dead and buried.

LE BEAU

There comes an old man and his three sons, —

CELIA

I could match this beginning with an old tale.

LE BEAU

Three proper young men, of excellent growth and
presence.

ROSALIND

With bills on their necks, 'Be it known unto all men by
these presents.'

LE BEAU

The eldest of the three wrestled with Charles, the duke's
wrestler; which Charles in a moment threw him, and
broke three of his ribs, that there is little hope of life in
him: so he served the second, and so the third. Yonder
they lie; the poor old man, their father, making such
pitiful dole over them, that all the beholders take his
part with weeping.

ROSALIND

Alas!

TOUCHSTONE

But what is the sport, monsieur, that the ladies have
lost?

LE BEAU

Why, this that I speak of.

TOUCHSTONE

Thus men may grow wiser every day! it is the first time
that ever I heard breaking of ribs was sport for ladies.

CELIA

Or I, I promise thee.

ROSALIND

But is there any else longs to see this broken music in his sides? is there yet another dotes upon rib-breaking? — Shall we see this wrestling, cousin?

LE BEAU

You must, if you stay here; for here is the place appointed for the wrestling, and they are ready to perform it.

CELIA

Yonder, sure, they are coming: let us now stay and see it.

Flourish. Enter DUKE FREDERICK, LORDS, ORLANDO, CHARLES, *and* ATTENDANTS.

DUKE FREDERICK

Come on: since the youth will not be entreated, his own peril on his forwardness.

ROSALIND

Is yonder the man?

LE BEAU

Even he, madam.

CELIA

Alas, he is too young! yet he looks successfully.

DUKE FREDERICK

How now, daughter, and cousin! are you crept hither to see the wrestling?

ROSALIND

Ay, my liege, so please you give us leave.

DUKE FREDERICK

You will take little delight in it, I can tell you, there is such odds in the men. In pity of the challenger's youth, I would fain dissuade him, but he will not be entreated. Speak to him, ladies; see if you can move him.

CELIA

Call him hither, good Monsieur Le Beau.

DUKE FREDERICK

Do so: I'll not be by.

LE BEAU

Monsieur the challenger, the princess call for you.

ORLANDO

I attend them with all respect and duty.

ROSALIND

Young man, have you challenged Charles the wrestler?

ORLANDO

No, fair princess; he is the general challenger: I come but in, as others do, to try with him the strength of my youth.

CELIA

Young gentleman, your spirits are too bold for your years. You have seen cruel proof of this man's strength: if you saw yourself with your eyes, or knew yourself with your judgement, the fear of your adventure would counsel you to a more equal enterprise. We pray you, for your own sake, to embrace your own safety, and give over this attempt.

ROSALIND

Do, young sir; your reputation shall not therefore be misprised: we will make it our suit to the duke that the wrestling might not go forward.

ORLANDO

I beseech you, punish me not with your hard thoughts: wherein I confess me much guilty, to deny so fair and excellent ladies any thing. But let your fair eyes and gentle wishes go with me to my trial; wherein if I be foil'd, there is but one shamed that was never gracious; if kill'd, but one dead that is willing to be so: I shall do my friends no wrong, for I have none to lament me; the world no injury, for in it I have nothing; only in the world I fill up a place, which may be better supplied when I have made it empty.

ROSALIND

The little strength that I have, I would it were with you.

CELIA

And mine, to eke out hers.

ROSALIND

Fare you well: pray heaven I be deceiv'd in you!

CELIA

Your heart's desires be with you!

CHARLES

Come, where is this young gallant that is so desirous to lie with his mother earth?

ORLANDO

Ready, sir; but his will hath in it a more modest working.

DUKE FREDERICK

You shall try but one fall.

CHARLES

No, I warrant your Grace, you shall not entreat him to a second, that have so mightily persuaded him from a first.

ORLANDO

An you mean to mock me after, you should not have mock'd me before: but come your ways.

ROSALIND

Now Hercules be thy speed, young man!

CELIA

I would I were invisible, to catch the strong fellow by the leg.   [*Wrestle.*

ROSALIND

O excellent young man!

CELIA

If I had a thunderbolt in mine eye, I can tell who should down.   [*Shout.* CHARLES *is thrown.*

DUKE FREDERICK

No more, no more.

ORLANDO

Yes, I beseech your Grace: I am not yet well breath'd.

DUKE FREDERICK

How dost thou, Charles?

LE BEAU

He cannot speak, my lord.

16

LE BEAU He cannot speak, my lord.

DUKE FREDERICK
  Bear him away. What is thy name, young man?
ORLANDO
  Orlando, my liege; the youngest son of Sir Rowland de
  Boys.
DUKE FREDERICK
  I would thou hadst been son to some man else:
  The world esteem'd thy father honourable,

But I did find him still mine enemy:
Thou shouldst have better pleas'd me with this deed,
Hadst thou descended from another house.
But fare thee well; thou art a gallant youth:
I would thou hadst told me of another father.

[*Exeunt* DUKE FREDERICK, TRAIN, *and* LE BEAU.

CELIA
Were I my father, coz, would I do this?

ORLANDO
I am more proud to be Sir Rowland's son,
His youngest son; — and would not change that calling,
To be adopted heir to Frederick.

ROSALIND
My father lov'd Sir Rowland as his soul,
And all the world was of my father's mind:
Had I before known this young man his son,
I should have given him tears unto entreaties,
Ere he should thus have ventur'd.

CELIA
                              Gentle cousin,
Let us go thank him and encourage him:
My father's rough and envious disposition
Sticks me at heart. — Sir, you have well deserv'd:
If you do keep your promises in love
But justly, as you have exceeded all promise,
Your mistress shall be happy.

ROSALIND
                              Gentleman,
                    [*Giving him a chain from her neck.*
Wear this for me, one out of suits with fortune,
That would give more, but that her hand lacks means.
— Shall we go, coz?

CELIA
                    Ay. — Fare you well, fair gentleman.

ORLANDO
Can I not say, I thank you? My better parts
Are all thrown down, and that which here stands up
Is but a quintain, a mere lifeless block.

18

ROSALIND

  He calls us back: my pride fell with my fortunes;
  I'll ask him what he would. — Did you call, sir? —
  Sir, you have wrestled well, and overthrown
  More than your enemies.

CELIA

                    Will you go, coz?

ROSALIND

  Have with you. — Fare you well.

                    [Exeunt ROSALIND and CELIA.

ORLANDO

  What passion hangs these weights upon my tongue?
  I cannot speak to her, yet she urg'd conference.
  O poor Orlando, thou art overthrown!
  Or Charles or something weaker masters thee.

                Enter LE BEAU.

LE BEAU

  Good sir, I do in friendship counsel you
  To leave this place. Albeit you have deserv'd
  High commendation, true applause and love,
  Yet such is now the duke's condition
  That he misconstrues all that you have done.
  The duke is humorous: what he is, indeed,
  More suits you to conceive than I to speak of.

ORLANDO

  I thank you, sir: and, pray you, tell me this, —
  Which of the two was daughter of the duke,
  That here was at the wrestling?

LE BEAU

  Neither his daughter, if we judge by manners;
  But yet, indeed, the smaller is his daughter:
  The other is daughter to the banish'd duke,
  And here detain'd by her usurping uncle,
  To keep his daughter company: whose loves
  Are dearer than the natural bond of sisters.
  But I can tell you that of late this duke
  Hath ta'en displeasure 'gainst his gentle niece,

Grounded upon no other argument
But that the people praise her for her virtues
And pity her for her good father's sake;
And, on my life, his malice 'gainst the lady
Will suddenly break forth. — Sir, fare you well:
Hereafter, in a better world than this,
I shall desire more love and knowledge of you.

ORLANDO

I rest much bounden to you: fare you well.

[*Exit* LE BEAU.

Thus must I from the smoke into the smother;
From tyrant duke unto a tyrant brother: —
But heavenly Rosalind!   [*Exit.*

SCENE III

A room in the palace.

Enter CELIA *and* ROSALIND.

Why, cousin; why, Rosalind; — Cupid have mercy! —
not a word?

ROSALIND

Not one to throw at a dog.

CELIA

No, thy words are too precious to be cast away upon
curs; throw some of them at me; come, lame me with
reasons.

ROSALIND

Then there were two cousins laid up, when the one
should be lamed with reasons, and the other mad
without any.

CELIA

But is all this for your father?

ROSALIND

No, some of it is for my father's child. O, how full of
briers is this working-day world!

CELIA

They are but burs, cousin, thrown upon thee in holiday
foolery: if we walk not in the trodden paths, our very
petticoats will catch them.

ROSALIND

I could shake them off my coat: these burs are in my
heart.

CELIA

Hem them away.

ROSALIND

I would try, if I could cry 'hem', and have him.

CELIA

Come, come, wrestle with thy affections.

ROSALIND

O, they take the part of a better wrestler than myself!

CELIA

O, a good wish upon you! you will try in time, in despite
of a fall. — But, turning these jests out of service, let us
talk in good earnest: is it possible, on such a sudden,
you should fall into so strong a liking with old Sir
Rowland's youngest son?

ROSALIND

The duke my father lov'd his father dearly.

CELIA

Doth it therefore ensue that you should love his son
dearly? By this kind of chase, I should hate him, for my
father hated his father dearly; yet I hate not Orlando.

ROSALIND

No, faith, hate him not, for my sake.

CELIA

Why should I? doth he not deserve well?

ROSALIND

Let me love him for that; and do you love him because I
do. — Look, here comes the duke.

CELIA

With his eyes full of anger.

Enter DUKE FREDERICK, *with* LORDS.

DUKE FREDERICK

Mistress, dispatch you with your safest haste,
And get you from our court.

ROSALIND

                    Me, uncle?

DUKE FREDERICK

                           You, cousin:

Within these ten days if that thou be'st found
So near our public court as twenty miles,
Thou diest for it.

ROSALIND

                I do beseech your Grace,

Let me the knowledge of my fault bear with me:
If with myself I hold intelligence,
Or have acquaintance with mine own desires;
If that I do not dream, or be not frantic,
As I do trust I am not, — then, dear uncle,
Never so much as in a thought unborn
Did I offend your highness.

DUKE FREDERICK

                    Thus do all traitors:

If their purgation did consist in words,
They are as innocent as grace itself:
Let it suffice thee that I trust thee not.

ROSALIND

Yet your mistrust cannot make me a traitor:
Tell me whereon the likelihood depends.

DUKE FREDERICK

Thou art thy father's daughter; there's enough.

ROSALIND

So was I when your highness took his dukedom;
So was I when your highness banish'd him:
Treason is not inherited, my lord;
Or, if we did derive it from our friends,
What's that to me? my father was no traitor:
Then, good my liege, mistake me not so much
To think my poverty is treacherous.

CELIA
  Dear sovereign, hear me speak.

DUKE FREDERICK
  Ay, Celia; we stay'd her for your sake,
  Else had she with her father rang'd along.

CELIA
  I did not then entreat to have her stay;
  It was your pleasure and your own remorse:
  I was too young that time to value her;
  But now I know her: if she be a traitor,
  Why, so am I; we still have slept together,
  Rose at an instant, learn'd, play'd, eat together;
  And wheresoe'er we went, like Juno's swans,
  Still we went coupled and inseparable.

DUKE FREDERICK
  She is too subtle for thee; and her smoothness,
  Her very silence and her patience
  Speak to the people, and they pity her.
  Thou art a fool: she robs thee of thy name;
  And thou wilt show more bright and seem more virtuous
  When she is gone. Then open not thy lips:
  Firm and irrevocable is my doom
  Which I have pass'd upon her; — she is banish'd.

CELIA
  Pronounce that sentence then on me, my liege:
  I cannot live out of her company.

DUKE FREDERICK
  You are a fool. — You, niece, provide yourself:
  If you outstay the time, upon mine honour,
  And in the greatness of my word, you die.

        [*Exeunt* DUKE FREDERICK *and* LORDS.

CELIA
  O my poor Rosalind! whither wilt thou go?
  Wilt thou change fathers? I will give thee mine.
  I charge thee, be not thou more griev'd than I am.

ROSALIND
  I have more cause.

CELIA
  Thou hast not, cousin;
  Prithee, be cheerful: know'st thou not, the duke
  Hath banish'd me, his daughter?
ROSALIND
                                    That he hath not.
CELIA
  No, hath not? Rosalind lacks then the love
  Which teacheth me that thou and I am one:
  Shall we be sunder'd? shall we part, sweet girl?
  No: let my father seek another heir.
  Therefore devise with me how we may fly,
  Whither to go and what to bear with us:
  And do not seek to takethe charge upon you,
  To bear your griefs yourself and leave me out:
  For, by this heaven, now at our sorrows pale,
  Say what thou canst, I'll go along with thee.
ROSALIND
  Why, whither shall we go?
CELIA
  To seek my uncle in the Forest of Arden.
ROSALIND
  Alas, what danger will it be to us,
  Maids as we are, to travel forth so far!
  Beauty provoketh thieves sooner than gold.
CELIA
  I'll put myself in poor and mean attire,
  And with a kind of umber smirch my face;
  The like do you: so shall we pass along
  And never stir assailants.
ROSALIND
                          Were it not better,
  Because that I am more than common tall,
  That I did suit me all points like a man?
  A gallant curtle-axe upon my thigh,
  A boar-spear in my hand; and — in my heart
  Lie there what hidden woman's fear there will —
  We'll have a swashing and a martial outside;

As many other mannish cowards have
That do outface it with their semblances.

CELIA

What shall I call thee when thou art a man?

ROSALIND

I'll have no worse a name than Jove's own page;
And therefore look you call me Ganymede.
But what will you be call'd?

CELIA

Something that hath a reference to my state;
No longer Celia, but Aliena.

ROSALIND

But, cousin, what if we assay'd to steal
The clownish fool out of your father's court?
Would he not be a comfort to our travel?

CELIA

He'll go along o'er the wide world with me;
Leave me alone to woo him. Let's away,
And get our jewels and our wealth together;
Devise the fittest time and safest way
To hide us from pursuit that will be made
After my flight. Now go we in content,
To liberty and not to banishment.   [*Exeunt.*

ACT II

SCENE I

The Forest of Arden.

Enter DUKE SENIOR, AMIENS, *and two or three*
LORDS, *like foresters.*

DUKE SENIOR

Now, my co-mates and brothers in exile,
Hath not old custom made this life more sweet
Than that of painted pomp? Are not these woods
More free from peril than the envious court?
Here feel we but the penalty of Adam,

The seasons' difference; as the icy fang
And churlish chiding of the winter's wind,
Which, when it bites and blows upon my body,
Even till I shrink with cold, I smile, and say:
'This is no flattery; these are counsellors
That feelingly persuade me what I am.'
Sweet are the uses of adversity;
Which, like the toad, ugly and venomous,
Wears yet a precious jewel in his head;
And this our life, exempt from public haunt,
Finds tongues in trees, books in the running brooks,
Sermons in stones, and good in every thing:
I would not change it.

AMIENS
                         Happy is your Grace,
That can translate the stubbornness of fortune
Into so quiet and so sweet a style.

DUKE SENIOR
Come, shall we go and kill us venison?
And yet it irks me the poor dappled fools,
Being native burghers of this desert city,
Should in their own confines with forked heads
Have their round haunches gored.

FIRST LORD
                                Indeed, my lord,
The melancholy Jaques grieves at that;
And, in that kind, swears you do more usurp
Than doth your brother that hath banish'd you.
To-day my Lord of Amiens and myself
Did steal behind him, as he lay along
Under an oak, whose antique root peeps out
Upon the brook that brawls along this wood:
To the which place a poor sequester'd stag,
That from the hunter's aim had ta'en a hurt,
Did come to languish; and, indeed, my lord,
The wretched animal heav'd forth such groans,
That their discharge did stretch his leathern coat
Almost to bursting; and the big round tears

26

Cours'd one another down his innocent nose
In piteous chase: and thus the hairy fool,
Much marked of the melancholy Jaques,
Stood on th'extremest verge of the swift brook,
Augmenting it with tears.

DUKE SENIOR
But what said Jaques?
Did he not moralise this spectacle?

FIRST LORD
O, yes, into a thousand similes.
First, for his weeping into the needless stream:
'Poor deer,' quoth he, 'thou makest a testament
As worldlings do, giving thy sum of more
To that which had too much': then, being there alone,
Left and abandon'd of his velvet friends,
''Tis right,' quoth he; 'thus misery doth part
The flux of company': anon, a careless herd,
Full of the pasture, jumps along by him,
And never stays to greet him: 'Ay,' quoth Jaques,
'Sweep on, you fat and greasy citizens;
'Tis just the fashion: wherefore do you look
Upon that poor and broken bankrupt there?'
Thus most invectively he pierceth through
The body of the country, city, court,
Yea, and of this our life: swearing that we
Are mere usurpers, tyrants, and what's worse,
To fright the animals, and to kill them up,
In their assign'd and native dwelling-place.

DUKE SENIOR
And did you leave him in this contemplation?

SECOND LORD
We did, my lord, weeping and commenting
Upon the sobbing deer.

DUKE SENIOR
                          Show me the place:
I love to cope him in these sullen fits,
For then he's full of matter.

FIRST LORD
I'll bring you to him straight.   [*Exeunt.*

SCENE II

A room in the palace.

Enter DUKE FREDERICK, *with* LORDS.

DUKE FREDERICK
Can it be possible that no man saw them?
It cannot be: some villains of my court
Are of consent and sufferance in this.

FIRST LORD
I cannot hear of any that did see her.
The ladies, her attendants of her chamber,
Saw her a-bed; and, in the morning early,
They found the bed untreasur'd of their mistress.

SECOND LORD
My lord, the roynish clown, at whom so oft
Your Grace was wont to laugh, is also missing.
Hesperia, the princess' gentlewoman,
Confesses that she secretly o'erheard
Your daughter and her cousin much commend
The parts and graces of the wrestler
That did but lately foil the sinewy Charles;
And she believes, wherever they are gone,
That youth is surely in their company.

DUKE FREDERICK
Send to his brother's; fetch that gallant hither:
If he be absent, bring his brother to me;
I'll make him find him: do this suddenly;
And let not search and inquisition quail
To bring again these foolish runaways.   [*Exeunt.*

28

SCENE III

Before OLIVER'S *house.*
Enter ORLANDO *and* ADAM, *meeting.*

ORLANDO
  Who's there?

ADAM
  What, my young master? O my gentle master!
  O my sweet master! O you memory
  Of old Sir Rowland! why, what make you here?
  Why are you virtuous? why do people love you?
  And wherefore are you gentle, strong and valiant?
  Why would you be so fond to overcome
  The bony priser of the humorous duke?
  Your praise is come too swiftly home before you.
  Know you not, master, to some kind of men
  Their graces serve them but as enemies?
  No more do yours: your virtues, gentle master,
  Are sanctified and holy traitors to you.
  O, what a world is this, when what is comely
  Envenoms him that bears it!

ORLANDO
  Why, what's the matter?

ADAM
                    O, unhappy youth!
  Come not within these doors; within this roof
  The enemy of all your Graces lives:
  Your brother — no, no brother; yet the son —
  Yet not the son, I will not call him son
  Of him I was about to call his father —
  Hath heard your praises; and this night he mean
  To burn the lodging where you use to lie,
  And you within it: if he fail of that,
  He will have other means to cut you off:
  I overheard him and his practices.
  This is no place; this house is but a butchery:
  Abhor it, fear it, do not enter it.

ORLANDO
Why, whither, Adam, wouldst thou have me go?
ADAM
No matter whither, so you come not here.
ORLANDO
What, wouldst thou have me go and beg my food?
Or with a base and boisterous sword enforce
A thievish living on the common road?
This I must do, or know not what to do:
Yet this I will not do, do how I can;
I rather will subject me to the malice
Of a diverted blood and bloody brother.
ADAM
But do not so. I have five hundred crowns,
The thrifty hire I sav'd under your father,
Which I did store to be my foster-nurse
When service should in my old limbs lie lame
And unregarded age in corners thrown:
Take that; and he that doth the ravens feed,
Yea, providently caters for the sparrow,
Be comfort to my age! Here is the gold;
All this I give you. Let me be your servant:
Though I look old, yet I am strong and lusty:
For in my youth I never did apply
Hot and rebellious liquors in my blood,
Nor did not with unbashful forehead woo
The means of weakness and debility;
Therefore my age is as a lusty winter,
Frosty, but kindly: let me go with you;
I'll do the service of a younger man
In all your business and necessities.
ORLANDO
O good old man, how well in thee appears
The constant service of the antique world,
When service sweat for duty, not for meed!
Thou art not for the fashion of these times,
Where none will sweat but for promotion,
And having that, do choke their service up

Even with the having: it is not so with thee.
But, poor old man, thou prunest a rotten tree,
That cannot so much as a blossom yield
In lieu of all thy pains and husbandry.
But come thy ways: we'll go along together;
And ere we have thy youthful wages spent,
We'll light upon some settled low content.

ADAM

Master, go on, and I will follow thee,
To the last gasp, with truth and loyalty.
From seventeen years till now almost fourscore
Here lived I, but now live here no more.
At seventeen years many their fortunes seek;
But at fourscore it is too late a week:
Yet fortune cannot recompense me better
Than to die well and not my master's debtor.   [Exeunt.

SCENE IV

The Forest of Arden.

Enter ROSALIND *for* GANYMEDE, CELIA *for*
ALIENA, *and* TOUCHSTONE.

ROSALIND

O Jupiter, how weary are my spirits!

TOUCHSTONE

I care not for my spirits, if my legs were not weary.

ROSALIND

I could find in my heart to disgrace my man's apparel
and to cry like a woman; but I must comfort the weaker
vessel, as doublet and hose ought to show itself
courageous to petticoat: therefore courage, good Aliena!

CELIA

I pray you, bear with me; I cannot go no further.

TOUCHSTONE

For my part, I had rather bear with you than bear you;
yet I should bear no cross, if I did bear you, for I think
you have no money in your purse.

ROSALIND

Well, this is the Forest of Arden.

TOUCHSTONE

Ay, now am I in Arden; the more fool I; when I was at home, I was in a better place: but travellers must be content.

ROSALIND

Ay, be so, good Touchstone.

Enter CORIN *and* SILVIUS.

Look you, who comes here; a young man and an old in solemn talk.

ROSALIND Well, this is the Forest of Arden.

CORIN

  That is the way to make her scorn you still.

SILVIUS

  O Corin, that thou knew'st how I do love her!

CORIN

  I partly guess; for I have lov'd ere now.

SILVIUS

  No, Corin, being old, thou canst not guess;
  Though in thy youth thou wast as true a lover
  As ever sigh'd upon a midnight pillow:
  But if thy love were ever like to mine, —
  As sure I think did never man love so, —
  How many actions most ridiculous
  Hast thou been drawn to by thy fantasy?

CORIN

  Into a thousand that I have forgotten.

SILVIUS

  O, thou didst then never love so heartily!
  If thou remember'st not the slightest folly
  That ever love did make thee run into,
  Thou hast not loved:
  Or if thou hast not sat as I do now,
  Wearing thy hearer in thy mistress' praise,
  Thou hast not loved:
  Or if thou hast not broke from company
  Abruptly, as my passion now makes me,
  Thou hast not loved.
  O Phebe, Phebe, Phebe!   [*Exit.*

ROSALIND

  Alas, poor shepherd! searching of thy wound, I have by
  hard adventure found mine own.

TOUCHSTONE

  And I mine. I remember, when I was in love I broke my
  sword upon a stone, and bid him take that for coming a-
  night to Jane Smile: and I remember the kissing of her
  batlet, and the cow's dugs that her pretty chopp'd hands
  had milk'd: and I remember the wooing of a peascod

instead of her; from whom I took two cods, and, giving her them again, said with weeping tears, 'Wear these for my sake.' We that are true lovers run into strange capers; but as all is mortal in nature, so is all nature in love mortal in folly.

ROSALIND

Thou speak'st wiser than thou art ware of.

TOUCHSTONE

Nay, I shall ne'er be ware of mine own wit till I break my shins against it.

ROSALIND

    Jove, Jove! this shepherd's passion
    Is much upon my fashion.

TOUCHSTONE

And mine; but it grows something stale with me.

CELIA

I pray you, one of you question yond man,
If he for gold will give us any food:
I faint almost to death.

TOUCHSTONE

           Holla, you clown!

ROSALIND

Peace, fool: he's not thy kinsman.

CORIN

                 Who calls?

TOUCHSTONE

Your betters, sir.

CORIN

Else are they very wretched.

ROSALIND

Peace, I say. — Good even to you, friend.

CORIN

And to you, gentle sir, and to you all.

ROSALIND

I prithee, shepherd, if that love or gold
Can in this desert place buy entertainment,

Bring us where we may rest ourselves and feed:
Here's a young maid with travel much oppress'd,
And faints for succour.

CORIN

               Fair sir, I pity her,
And wish, for her sake more than for mine own,
My fortunes were more able to relieve her;
But I am shepherd to another man
And do not shear the fleeces that I graze:
My master is of churlish disposition,
And little recks to find the way to heaven
By doing deeds of hospitality:
Besides, his cote, his flocks, and bounds of feed,
Are now on sale; and at our sheepcote now,
By reason of his absence, there is nothing
That you will feed on; but what is, come see,
And in my voice most welcome shall you be.

ROSALIND

What is he that shall buy his flock and pasture?

CORIN

That young swain that you saw here but erewhile,
That little cares for buying any thing.

ROSALIND

I pray thee, if it stand with honesty,
Buy thou the cottage, pasture, and the flock,
And thou shalt have to pay for it of us.

CELIA

And we will mend thy wages. I like this place,
And willingly could waste my time in it.

CORIN

Assuredly the thing is to be sold:
Go with me: if you like, upon report,
The soil, the profit, and this kind of life,
I will your very faithful feeder be,
And buy it with your gold right suddenly.   [*Exeunt.*

SCENE V

The forest.

Enter AMIENS, JAQUES, *and others.*

AMIENS [*sings*].

> Under the greenwood tree
>   Who loves to lie with me,
> And turn his merry note
>   Unto the sweet bird's throat,
> Come hither, come hither, come hither:
>   Here shall he see
>   No enemy
> But winter and rough weather.

JAQUES

More, more, I prithee, more.

AMIENS

It will make you melancholy, Monsieur Jaques.

JAQUES

I thank it. More, I prithee, more. I can suck melancholy out of a song, as a weasel sucks eggs. More, I prithee, more.

AMIENS

My voice is ragged: I know I cannot please you.

JAQUES

I do not desire you to please me; I do desire you to sing. Come, more; another stanzo: call you 'em stanzos?

AMIENS

What you will, Monsieur Jaques.

JAQUES

Nay, I care not for their names; they owe me nothing. Will you sing?

AMIENS

More at your request than to please myself.

JAQUES

Well, then, if ever I thank any man, I'll thank you: but that they call compliment is like th'encounter of two

36

dog-apes; and when a man thanks me heartily, methinks
I have given him a penny and he renders me the
beggarly thanks. Come, sing; and you that will not, hold
your tongues.

AMIENS

Well, I'll end the song. — Sirs, cover the while; the duke
will drink under this tree. — He hath been all this day to
look you.

JAQUES

And I have been all this day to avoid him. He is too
disputable for my company: I think of as many matters
as he; but I give heaven thanks, and make no boast of
them. Come, warble, come.

> *Song.*
>
> Who doth ambition shun   [*All together here.*
> And loves to live i'th'sun,
> Seeking the food he eats
> And pleased with what he gets,
> Come hither, come hither, come hither:
> Here shall he see
> No enemy
> But winter and rough weather.

JAQUES

I'll give you a verse to this note, that I made yesterday in
despite of my invention.

AMIENS

And I'll sing it.

JAQUES

Thus it goes: —

> If it do come to pass
> That any man turn ass,
> Leaving his wealth and ease,
> A stubborn will to please,
> Ducdame, ducdame, ducdame:
> Here shall he see
> Gross fools as he,
> An if he will come to me.

AMIENS
  What's that 'ducdame'?

JAQUES
  'Tis a Greek invocation, to call fools into a circle.
  I'll go sleep, if I can; if I cannot, I'll rail against
  all the first-born of Egypt.

AMIENS
  And I'll go seek the duke: his banquet is prepared.
                                        [Exeunt severally.

SCENE VI

The forest.

Enter ORLANDO *and* ADAM.

ADAM
  Dear master, I can go no further: O, I die for food! Here
  lie I down, and measure out my grave. Farewell, kind
  master.

ORLANDO
  Why, how now, Adam! no greater heart in thee? Live a
  little; comfort a little; cheer thyself a little. If this uncouth
  forest yield any thing savage, I will either be food for it or
  bring it for food to thee. Thy conceit is nearer death than
  thy powers. For my sake be comfortable; hold death
  awhile at the arm's end: I will here be with thee presently;
  and if I bring thee not something to eat, I will give thee
  leave to die: but if thou diest before I come, thou art a
  mocker of my labour. Well said! thou look'st cheerly; and
  I'll be with thee quickly. Yet thou liest in the bleak air:
  come, I will bear thee to some shelter; and thou shalt not
  die for lack of a dinner, if there live any thing in this desert.
  Cheerly, good Adam!   [Exeunt.

SCENE VII

The forest. A table set out.

Enter DUKE SENIOR, AMIENS, *and* LORDS *like*
OUTLAWS.

DUKE SENIOR
  I think he be transform'd into a beast;
  For I can no where find him like a man.

FIRST LORD
  My lord, he is but even now gone hence:
  Here was he merry, hearing of a song.

DUKE SENIOR
  If he, compact of jars, grow musical,
  We shall have shortly discord in the spheres.
  Go, seek him: tell him I would speak with him.

Enter JAQUES.

FIRST LORD
  He saves my labour by his own approach.

DUKE SENIOR
  Why, how now, monsieur! what a life is this,
  That your poor friends must woo your company!
  What, you look merrily!

JAQUES
  A fool, a fool! I met a fool i'th'forest,
  A motley fool; a miserable world!
  As I do live by food, I met a fool;
  Who laid him down and bask'd him in the sun,
  And rail'd on Lady Fortune in good terms,
  In good set terms, and yet a motley fool.
  'Good morrow, fool,' quoth I. 'No, sir,' quoth he,
  'Call me not fool till heaven hath sent me fortune':
  And then he drew a dial from his poke,
  And, looking on it with lack-lustre eye,
  Says very wisely, 'It is ten o'clock:
  Thus we may see,' quoth he, 'how the world wags:
  'Tis but an hour ago since it was nine,

And after one hour more 'twill be eleven;
And so, from hour to hour, we ripe and ripe,
And then, from hour to hour, we rot and rot;
And thereby hangs a tale.' When I did hear
The motley fool thus moral on the time,
My lungs began to crow like chanticleer,
That fools should be so deep-contemplative;
And I did laugh sans intermission
An hour by his dial. O noble fool!
A worthy fool! Motley's the only wear.

DUKE SENIOR
  What fool is this?

JAQUES
  O worthy fool! One that hath been a courtier;
  And says, if ladies be but young and fair,
  They have the gift to know it: and in his brain, —
  Which is as dry as the remainder biscuit
  After a voyage, — he hath strange places cramm'd
  With observation, the which he vents
  In mangled forms. — O, that I were a fool!
  I am ambitious for a motley coat.

DUKE SENIOR
  Thou shalt have one.

JAQUES
                      It is my only suit;
Provided that you weed your better judgements
Of all opinion that grows rank in them
That I am wise. I must have liberty
Withal, as large a charter as the wind,
To blow on whom I please; for so fools have:
And they that are most galled with my folly,
They most must laugh. And why, sir, must they so?
The 'why' is plain as way to parish church:
He that a fool doth very wisely hit
Doth very foolishly, although he smart,
Not to seem senseless of the bob: if not,
The wise man's folly is anatomis'd
Even by the squandering glances of the fool.

Invest me in my motley; give me leave
To speak my mind, and I will through and through
Cleanse the foul body of th'infected world,
If they will patiently receive my medicine.

DUKE SENIOR

Fie on thee! I can tell what thou wouldst do.

JAQUES

What, for a counter, would I do but good?

DUKE SENIOR

Most mischievous foul sin, in chiding sin:
For thou thyself hast been a libertine,
As sensual as the brutish sting itself;
And all th'imbossed sores and headed evils,
That thou with licence of free foot hast caught,
Wouldst thou disgorge into the general world.

JAQUES

Why, who cries out on pride,
That can therein tax any private party?
Doth it not flow as hugely as the sea,
Till that the weary very waves do ebb?
What woman in the city do I name,
When that I say the city-woman bears
The cost of princes on unworthy shoulders?
Who can come in and say that I mean her,
When such a one as she such is her neighbour?
Or what is he of basest function,
That says his bravery is not on my cost,
Thinking that I mean him, but therein suits
His folly to the mettle of my speech?
There then; how then? what then? Let me see wherein
My tongue hath wrong'd him: if it do him right,
Then he hath wrong'd himself; if he be free,
Why, then my taxing like a wild-goose flies,
Unclaim'd of any man. — But who comes here?

Enter ORLANDO, *with his sword drawn.*

ORLANDO

Forbear, and eat no more!

JAQUES

                    Why, I have eat none yet.

ORLANDO
  Nor shalt not, till necessity be served.

JAQUES
  Of what kind should this cock come of?

DUKE SENIOR
  Art thou thus bolden'd, man, by thy distress,
  Or else a rude despiser of good manners,
  That in civility thou seem'st so empty?

ORLANDO
  You touch'd my vein at first: the thorny point
  Of bare distress hath ta'en from me the show
  Of smooth civility: yet am I inland bred,
  And know some nurture. But forbear, I say:
  He dies that touches any of this fruit
  Till I and my affairs are answered.

JAQUES
  An you will not be answer'd with reason, I must die.

DUKE SENIOR
  What would you have? Your gentleness shall force
  More than your force move us to gentleness.

ORLANDO
  I almost die for food; and let me have it.

DUKE SENIOR
  Sit down and feed, and welcome to our table.

ORLANDO
  Speak you so gently? Pardon me, I pray you:
  I thought that all things had been savage here;
  And therefore put I on the countenance
  Of stern commandment. But whate'er you are,
  That in this desert inaccessible,
  Under the shade of melancholy boughs,
  Lose and neglect the creeping hours of time;
  If ever you have look'd on better days,
  If ever been where bells have knoll'd to church,
  If ever sat at any good man's feast,

If ever from your eyelids wip'd a tear,
And know what 'tis to pity and be pitied, —
Let gentleness my strong enforcement be:
In the which hope I blush, and hide my sword.

DUKE SENIOR
True is it that we have seen better days,
And have with holy bell been knoll'd to church,
And sat at good men's feasts, and wip'd our eyes
Of drops that sacred pity hath engender'd:
And therefore sit you down in gentleness,
And take upon command what help we have,
That to your wanting may be minister'd.

ORLANDO
Then but forbear your food a little while,
Whiles, like a doe, I go to find my fawn,
And give it food. There is an old poor man,
Who after me hath many a weary step
Limp'd in pure love: till he be first sufficed, —
Oppress'd with two weak evils, age and hunger, —
I will not touch a bit.

DUKE SENIOR
                    Go find him out,
And we will nothing waste till you return.

ORLANDO
I thank ye; and be blest for your good comfort!   [*Exit.*

DUKE SENIOR
Thou seest we are not all alone unhappy:
This wide and universal theatre
Presents more woeful pageants than the scene
Wherein we play in.

JAQUES
                    All the world's a stage,
And all the men and women merely players:
They have their exits and their entrances;
And one man in his time plays many parts,
His acts being seven ages. As, first the infant,
Mewling and puking in the nurse's arms.
And then the whining schoolboy, with his satchel

And shining morning face, creeping like snail
Unwillingly to school. And then the lover,
Sighing like furnace, with a woeful ballad
Made to his mistress' eyebrow. Then the soldier,
Full of strange oaths, and bearded like the pard,
Jealous in honour, sudden and quick in quarrel,
Seeking the bubble reputation
Even in the cannon's mouth. And then the justice,
In fair round belly with good capon lined,
With eyes severe and beard of formal cut,
Full of wise saws and modern instances;
And so he plays his part. The sixth age shifts
Into the lean and slipper'd pantaloon,
With spectacles on nose and pouch on side;
His youthful hose, well sav'd, a world too wide
For his shrunk shank; and his big manly voice,
Turning again toward childish treble, pipes
And whistles in his sound. Last scene of all,
That ends this strange eventful history,
Is second childishness and mere oblivion,
Sans teeth, sans eyes, sans taste, sans everything.

Enter ORLANDO, *with* ADAM.

DUKE SENIOR
  Welcome. Set down your venerable burthen,
  And let him feed.

ORLANDO
  I thank you most for him.

ADAM
               So had you need: —
  I scarce can speak to thank you for myself.

DUKE SENIOR
  Welcome; fall to: I will not trouble you
  As yet, to question you about your fortunes. —
  Give us some music; and, good cousin, sing.

AMIENS
      Blow, blow, thou winter wind,
      Thou art not so unkind

As man's ingratitude;
   Thy tooth is not so keen,
   Because thou art not seen,
     Although thy breath be rude.
Heigh-ho! sing, heigh-ho! unto the green holly:
Most friendship is feigning, most loving mere folly:
     Then, heigh-ho, the holly!
       This life is most jolly.

   Freeze, freeze, thou bitter sky,
   That dost not bite so nigh
     As benefits forgot:
   Though thou the waters warp,
   Thy sting is not so sharp
     As friend remember'd not.
Heigh-ho! Sing, heigh-ho! *etc.*

DUKE SENIOR
If that you were the good Sir Rowland's son,
As you have whisper'd faithfully you were,
And as mine eye doth his effigies witness
Most truly limn'd and living in your face, —
Be truly welcome hither: I am the duke,
That lov'd your father: the residue of your fortune,
Go to my cave and tell me. — Good old man,
Thou art right welcome as thy master is. —
Support him by the arm. — Give me your hand,
And let me all your fortunes understand.   [*Exeunt.*

ACT III

SCENE I

A room in the palace.

Enter DUKE FREDERICK, LORDS, *and* OLIVER.

DUKE FREDERICK
Not see him since? Sir, sir, that cannot be:
But were I not the better part made mercy,

I should not seek an absent argument
Of my revenge, thou present. But look to it:
Find out thy brother, wheresoe'er he is;
Seek him with candle; bring him dead or living
Within this twelvemonth, or turn thou no more
To seek a living in our territory.
Thy lands, and all things that thou dost call thine
Worth seizure, do we seize into our hands,
Till thou canst quit thee by thy brother's mouth
Of what we think against thee.

OLIVER

O, that your highness knew my heart in this!
I never lov'd my brother in my life.

DUKE FREDERICK

More villain thou. — Well, push him out of doors;
And let my officers of such a nature
Make an extent upon his house and lands:
Do this expediently, and turn him going.   [*Exeunt.*

DUKE FREDERICK Find out thy brother, wheresoe'er he is.

46

SCENE II

The forest.
Enter ORLANDO, *with a paper.*

ORLANDO

Hang there, my verse, in witness of my love:
And thou, thrice-crowned queen of night, survey
With thy chaste eye, from thy pale sphere above,
   Thy huntress' name, that my full life doth sway.
O Rosalind! these trees shall be my books,
   And in their barks my thoughts I'll character;
That every eye, which in this forest looks,
   Shall see thy virtue witness'd every where.
Run, run, Orlando; carve on every tree
The fair, the chaste, and unexpressive she.

                          [*Exit.*

Enter CORIN *and* TOUCHSTONE.

CORIN

And how like you this shepherd's life, Master
  Touchstone?

TOUCHSTONE

Truly, shepherd, in respect of itself, it is a good life; but
in respect that it is a shepherd's life, it is naught. In
respect that it is solitary, I like it very well; but in respect
that it is private, it is a very vile life. Now, in respect it is
in the fields, it pleaseth me well; but in respect it is not
in the court, it is tedious. As it is a spare life, look you, it
fits my humour well; but as there is no more plenty in it,
it goes much against my stomach. Hast any philosophy
in thee, shepherd?

CORIN

No more but that I know the more one sickens the
worse at ease he is; and that he that wants money,
means, and content, is without three good friends; that
the property of rain is to wet, and fire to burn; that good
pasture makes fat sheep; and that a great cause of the
night is lack of the sun; that he that hath learn'd no wit

by nature nor art may complain of good breeding, or comes of a very dull kindred.

TOUCHSTONE

Such a one is a natural philosopher. Wast ever in court, shepherd?

CORIN

No, truly.

TOUCHSTONE

Then thou art damn'd.

CORIN

Nay, I hope, —

TOUCHSTONE Such a one is a natural philosopher.

TOUCHSTONE

Truly, thou art damn'd; like an ill-roasted egg, all on one side.

CORIN

For not being at court? Your reason?

TOUCHSTONE

Why, if thou never wast at court, thou never saw'st good manners; if thou never saw'st good manners, then thy manners must be wicked; and wickedness is sin, and sin is damnation. Thou art in a parlous state, shepherd.

CORIN

Not a whit, Touchstone: those that are good manners at the court, are as ridiculous in the country as the behaviour of the country is most mockable at the court. You told me you salute not at the court, but you kiss your hands: that courtesy would be uncleanly, if courtiers were shepherds.

TOUCHSTONE

Instance, briefly; come, instance.

CORIN

Why, we are still handling our ewes; and their fells, you know, are greasy.

TOUCHSTONE

Why, do not your courtier's hands sweat? and is not the grease of a mutton as wholesome as the sweat of a man? Shallow, shallow. A better instance, I say; come.

CORIN

Besides, our hands are hard.

TOUCHSTONE

Your lips will feel them the sooner. Shallow again. A more sounder instance, come.

CORIN

And they are often tarr'd over with the surgery of our sheep; and would you have us kiss tar? The courtier's hands are perfumed with civet.

TOUCHSTONE

Most shallow man! thou worms-meat, in respect of a
good piece of flesh, indeed! — Learn of the wise, and
perpend: civet is of a baser birth than tar, — the very
uncleanly flux of a cat. Mend the instance, shepherd.

CORIN

You have too courtly a wit for me: I'll rest.

TOUCHSTONE

Wilt thou rest damn'd? God help thee, shallow man!
God make incision in thee! thou art raw.

CORIN

Sir, I am a true labourer: I earn that I eat, get that I
wear; owe no man hate, envy no man's happiness; glad
of other men's good, content with my harm; and the
greatest of my pride is, to see my ewes graze and my
lambs suck.

TOUCHSTONE

That is another simple sin in you; to bring the ewes
and the rams together, and to offer to get your living by
the copulation of cattle; to be bawd to a bell-wether; and
to betray a she-lamb of a twelvemonth to a crooked-
pated, old, cuckoldly ram, out of all reasonable match.
If thou be'st not damn'd for this, the devil himself will
have no shepherds; I cannot see else how thou shouldst
scape.

CORIN

Here comes young Master Ganymede, my new
mistress's brother.

     Enter ROSALIND, *with a paper, reading.*

ROSALIND

    From the east to western Ind,
    No jewel is like Rosalind.
    Her worth, being mounted on the wind,
    Through all the world bears Rosalind.
    All the pictures fairest lin'd
    Are but black to Rosalind.
    Let no face be kept in mind

But the fair of Rosalind.

TOUCHSTONE

I'll rime you so eight years together, dinners and suppers
and sleeping-hours excepted: it is the right butter-
women's rank to market.

ROSALIND

Out, fool!

TOUCHSTONE

For a taste:

> If a hart do lack a hind,
> Let him seek out Rosalind.
> If the cat will after kind,
> So be sure will Rosalind.
> Winter garments must be lin'd,
> So must slender Rosalind.
> They that reap must sheaf and bind;
> Then to cart with Rosalind.
> Sweetest nut hath sourest rind,
> Such a nut is Rosalind.
> He that sweetest rose will find,
> Must find love's prick and Rosalind.

This is the very false gallop of verses: why do you
infect yourself with them?

ROSALIND

Peace, you dull fool! I found them on a tree.

TOUCHSTONE

Truly, the tree yields bad fruit.

ROSALIND

I'll graff it with you, and then I shall graff it with a
meddler: then it will be the earliest fruit i'th'country; for
you'll be rotten ere you be half ripe, and that's the right
virtue of the medlar.

TOUCHSTONE

You have said; but whether wisely or no, let the forest
judge.

Enter CELIA, *with a writing.*

TOUCHSTONE Truly, the tree yields bad fruit.

ROSALIND
  Peace!
  Here comes my sister, reading: stand aside.
CELIA [reads].
    Why should this a desert be?
      For it is unpeopled? No;
    Tongues I'll hang on every tree,
      That shall civil sayings show:
    Some, how brief the life of man
      Runs his erring pilgrimage,
    That the stretching of a span

Buckles in his sum of age;
Some, of violated vows
'Twixt the souls of friend and friend:
But upon the fairest boughs,
Or at every sentence end,
Will I Rosalinda write;
Teaching all that read to know
The quintessence of every sprite
Heaven would in little show.
Therefore Heaven Nature charged
That one body should be fill'd
With all graces wide-enlarged:
Nature presently distill'd
Helen's cheek, but not her heart;
Cleopatra's majesty;
Atalanta's better part;
Sad Lucretia's modesty.
Thus Rosalind of many parts
By heavenly synod was devised;
Of many faces, eyes, and hearts,
To have the touches dearest prized.
Heaven would that she these gifts should have,
And I to live and die her slave.

ROSALIND

O most gentle pulpiter! — what tedious homily of love
have you wearied your parishioners withal, and never
cried, 'Have patience, good people!'

CELIA

How now! back, friends: — shepherd, go off a little: —
go with him, sirrah.

TOUCHSTONE

Come, shepherd, let us make an honourable retreat;
though not with bag and baggage, yet with scrip and
scrippage.

[*Exeunt* CORIN *and* TOUCHSTONE.

CELIA

Didst thou hear these verses?

ROSALIND

O, yes, I heard them all, and more too; for some of them had in them more feet than the verses would bear.

CELIA

That's no matter: the feet might bear the verses.

ROSALIND

Ay, but the feet were lame, and could not bear themselves without the verse, and therefore stood lamely in the verse.

CELIA

But didst thou hear without wondering how thy name should be hang'd and carved upon these trees?

ROSALIND

I was seven of the nine days out of the wonder before you came; for look here what I found on a palm-tree: — I was never so berimed since Pythagoras' time, that I was an Irish rat, which I can hardly remember.

CELIA

Trow you who hath done this?

ROSALIND

Is it a man?

CELIA

And a chain, that you once wore, about his neck. Change you colour?

ROSALIND

I prithee, who?

CELIA

O Lord, Lord! it is a hard matter for friends to meet; but mountains may be removed with earthquakes and so encounter.

ROSALIND

Nay, but who is it?

CELIA

Is it possible?

ROSALIND

Nay, I prithee now with most petitionary vehemence, tell me who it is.

CELIA

O wonderful, wonderful, and most wonderful
wonderful! and yet again wonderful, and after that, out
of all whooping!

ROSALIND

Good my complexion! dost thou think, though I am
caparison'd like a man, I have a doublet and hose in my
disposition? One inch of delay more is a South-sea of
discovery; I prithee, tell me who is it quickly, and speak
apace. I would thou couldst stammer, that thou
mightest pour this conceal'd man out of thy mouth, as
wine comes out of a narrow-mouth'd bottle, — either
too much at once, or none at all. I prithee, take the cork
out of thy mouth, that I may drink thy tidings.

CELIA

So you may put a man in your belly.

ROSALIND

Is he of God's making? What manner of man? Is his
head worth a hat, or his chin worth a beard?

CELIA

Nay, he hath but a little beard.

ROSALIND

Why, God will send more, if the man will be thankful:
let me stay the growth of his beard, if thou delay me not
the knowledge of his chin.

CELIA

It is young Orlando, that tripp'd up the wrestler's heels
and your heart both in an instant.

ROSALIND

Nay, but the devil take mocking: speak, sad brow and
true maid.

CELIA

I'faith, coz, 'tis he.

ROSALIND

Orlando?

CELIA

Orlando.

ROSALIND

Alas the day! what shall I do with my doublet and hose?
— What did he when thou saw'st him? What said he?
How look'd he? Wherein went he? What makes he here?
Did he ask for me? Where remains he? How parted he
with thee? and when shalt thou see him again? Answer
me in one word.

CELIA

You must borrow me Gargantua's mouth first: 'tis a
word too great for any mouth of this age's size. To say
ay and no to these particulars is more than to answer in
a catechism.

ROSALIND

But doth he know that I am in this forest, and in man's
apparel? Looks he as freshly as he did the day he
wrestled?

CELIA

It is as easy to count atomies as to resolve the
propositions of a lover: — but take a taste of my finding
him, and relish it with good observance. I found him
under a tree, like a dropp'd acorn.

ROSALIND

It may well be call'd Jove's tree, when it drops forth
such fruit.

CELIA

Give me audience, good madam.

ROSALIND

Proceed.

CELIA

There lay he, stretch'd along, like a wounded knight.

ROSALIND

Though it be pity to see such a sight, it well becomes the
ground.

CELIA

Cry, holla! to thy tongue, I prithee; it curvets
unseasonably. He was furnish'd like a hunter.

ROSALIND

O, ominous, he comes to kill my heart.

CELIA

I would sing my song without a burden: thou bring'st
me out of tune.

ROSALIND

Do you not know I am a woman? when I think, I must
speak. Sweet, say on.

CELIA

You bring me out. — Soft! comes he not here?

ROSALIND

'Tis he: slink by, and note him.

[CELIA and ROSALIND retire.

Enter ORLANDO and JAQUES.

JAQUES

I thank you for your company; but, good faith, I had as
lief have been myself alone.

ORLANDO

And so had I; but yet, for fashion sake,
I thank you too for your society.

JAQUES

God b' wi' you! let's meet as little as we can.

ORLANDO

I do desire we may be better strangers.

JAQUES

I pray you, mar no more trees with writing love-songs in
their barks.

ORLANDO

I pray you, mar no more of my verses with reading them
ill-favour'dly.

JAQUES

Rosalind is your love's name?

ORLANDO

Yes, just.

JAQUES

I do not like her name.

ORLANDO
  There was no thought of pleasing you when she was
  christen'd.

JAQUES
  What stature is she of?

ORLANDO
  Just as high as my heart.

JAQUES
  You are full of pretty answers. Have you not been
  acquainted with goldsmiths' wives, and conn'd them
  out of rings?

ORLANDO
  Not so; but I answer you right painted cloth, from
  whence you have studied your questions.

JAQUES
  You have a nimble wit: I think 'twas made of Atalanta's
  heels. Will you sit down with me? and we two will rail
  against our mistress the world and all our misery.

ORLANDO
  I will chide no breather in the world but myself, against
  whom I know most faults.

JAQUES
  The worst fault you have is to be in love.

ORLANDO
  'Tis a fault I will not change for your best virtue.
  I am weary of you.

JAQUES
  By my troth, I was seeking for a fool when I found you.

ORLANDO
  He is drown'd in the brook: look but in, and you shall
  see him.

JAQUES
  There I shall see mine own figure.

ORLANDO
  Which I take to be either a fool or a cipher.

JAQUES
  I'll tarry no longer with you: farewell, good Signior Love.

ORLANDO

I am glad of your departure: adieu, good Monsieur
Melancholy.

[*Exit* JAQUES, CELIA *and* ROSALIND
come forward.

ROSALIND [*aside to* CELIA].

I will speak to him like a saucy lackey, and under that
habit play the knave with him. — Do you hear, forester?

ORLANDO

Very well: what would you?

ROSALIND

I pray you, what is't o'clock?

ORLANDO

You should ask me, what time o'day: there's no clock in
the forest.

ROSALIND

Then there is no true lover in the forest; else sighing
every minute, and groaning every hour, would detect the
lazy foot of Time as well as a clock.

ORLANDO

And why not the swift foot of Time? had not that been
as proper?

ROSALIND

By no means, sir. Time travels in divers paces with
divers persons: I'll tell you who Time ambles withal,
who Time trots withal, who Time gallops withal, and
who he stands still withal.

ORLANDO

I prithee, who doth he trot withal?

ROSALIND

Marry, he trots hard with a young maid between the
contract of her marriage and the day it is solemnised:
if the interim be but a se'nnight, Time's pace is so hard
that it seems the length of seven year.

ORLANDO

Who ambles Time withal?

ROSALIND
With a priest that lacks Latin, and a rich man that hath
not the gout; for the one sleeps easily, because he cannot
study; and the other lives merrily, because he feels no
pain: the one lacking the burden of lean and wasteful
learning; the other knowing no burthen of heavy tedious
penury: these Time ambles withal.

ORLANDO
Who doth he gallop withal?

ROSALIND
With a thief to the gallows; for though he go as softly as
foot can fall, he thinks himself too soon there.

ORLANDO
Who stays it still withal?

ROSALIND
With lawyers in the vacation; for they sleep between
term and term, and then they perceive not how Time
moves.

ORLANDO
Where dwell you, pretty youth?

ROSALIND
With this shepherdess, my sister; here in the skirts of the
forest, like fringe upon a petticoat.

ORLANDO
Are you native of this place?

ROSALIND
As the cony, that you see dwell where she is kindled.

ORLANDO
Your accent is something finer than you could purchase
in so removed a dwelling.

ROSALIND
I have been told so of many: but indeed an old religious
uncle of mine taught me to speak, who was in his youth
an inland man; one that knew courtship too well, for
there he fell in love. I have heard him read many
lectures against it; and I thank God I am not a woman,

to be touch'd with so many giddy offences as he hath
generally taxed their whole sex withal.

ORLANDO

Can you remember any of the principal evils that he laid
to the charge of women?

ROSALIND

There were none principal: they were all like one
another as half-pence are; every one fault seeming
monstrous till his fellow-fault came to match it.

ORLANDO

I prithee, recount some of them.

ROSALIND

No, I will not cast away my physic but on those that are
sick. There is a man haunts the forest, that abuses our
young plants with carving Rosalind on their barks; hangs
odes upon hawthorns, and elegies on brambles; all,
forsooth, deifying the name of Rosalind: if I could meet
that fancy-monger, I would give him some good
counsel, for he seems to have the quotidian of love upon
him.

ORLANDO

I am he that is so love-shaked: I pray you, tell me
your remedy.

ROSALIND

There is none of my uncle's marks upon you: he taught
me how to know a man in love; in which cage of rushes I
am sure you are not prisoner.

ORLANDO

What were his marks?

ROSALIND

A lean cheek, — which you have not; a blue eye and
sunken, — which you have not; an unquestionable
spirit, — which you have not; a beard neglected, —
which you have not; — but I pardon you for that; for
simply your having in beard is a younger brother's
revenue: — then your hose should be ungarter'd, your
bonnet unbanded, your sleeve unbutton'd, your shoe

untied, and every thing about you demonstrating a careless desolation; — but you are no such man, — you are rather point-device in your accoutrements, as loving yourself than seeming the lover of any other.

ORLANDO

Fair youth, I would I could make thee believe I love.

ROSALIND

Me believe it! you may as soon make her that you love believe it; which, I warrant, she is apter to do than to confess she does: that is one of the points in which women still give the lie to their consciences. But, in good sooth, are you he that hangs the verses on the trees, wherein Rosalind is so admired?

ORLANDO

I swear to thee, youth, by the white hand of Rosalind, I am that he, that unfortunate he.

ROSALIND

But are you so much in love as your rimes speak?

ORLANDO

Neither rime nor reason can express how much.

ROSALIND

Love is merely a madness; and, I tell you, deserves as well a dark house and a whip as madmen do: and the reason why they are not so punish'd and cured is, that the lunacy is so ordinary, that the whippers are in love too. Yet I profess curing it by counsel.

ORLANDO

Did you ever cure any so?

ROSALIND

Yes, one; and in this manner. He was to imagine me his love, his mistress; and I set him every day to woo me: at which time would I, being but a moonish youth, grieve, be effeminate, changeable, longing, and liking; proud, fantastical, apish, shallow, inconstant, full of tears, full of smiles; for every passion something, and for no passion truly any thing, as boys and women are for the most part cattle of this colour: would now like him, now

loathe him; then entertain him, then forswear him; now
weep for him, then spit at him; that I drave my suitor
from his mad humour of love to a living humour of
madness; which was, to forswear the full stream of the
world, and to live in a nook merely monastic. And thus I
cured him; and this way will I take upon me to wash
your liver as clean as a sound sheep's heart, that there
shall not be one spot of love in't.

ORLANDO

I would not be cured, youth.

ROSALIND

I would cure you, if you would but call me Rosalind,
and come every day to my cote and woo me.

ORLANDO

Now, by the faith of my love, I will: tell me where it is.

ROSALIND

Go with me to it, and I'll show it you: and, by the way,
you shall tell me where in the forest you live. Will you
go?

ORLANDO

With all my heart, good youth.

ROSALIND

Nay, you must call me Rosalind. — Come, sister, will you
go?   [Exeunt.

SCENE III

The forest.

Enter TOUCHSTONE *and* AUDREY; JAQUES *behind.*

TOUCHSTONE

Come apace, good Audrey: I will fetch up your goats,
Audrey. And how, Audrey? am I the man yet? doth my
simple feature content you?

AUDREY

Your features! Lord warrant us! what features?

TOUCHSTONE

I am here with thee and thy goats, as the most
capricious poet, honest Ovid, was among the Goths.

JAQUES [*aside*].

O knowledge ill-inhabited, — worse than Jove in a
thatch'd house!

TOUCHSTONE

When a man's verses cannot be understood, nor a man's
good wit seconded with the forward child
Understanding, it strikes a man more dead than a great
reckoning in a little room. — Truly, I would the gods
had made thee poetical.

AUDREY

I do not know what 'poetical' is: is it honest in deed and
word? is it a true thing?

TOUCHSTONE

No, truly; for the truest poetry is the most feigning; and
lovers are given to poetry; and what they swear in poetry
may be said as lovers they do feign.

AUDREY

Do you wish, then, that the gods had made me poetical?

TOUCHSTONE

I do, truly; for thou swear'st to me thou art honest: now, if
thou wert a poet, I might have some hope thou didst feign.

AUDREY

Would you not have me honest?

TOUCHSTONE

No, truly, unless thou wert hard-favour'd; for honesty
coupled to beauty is to have honey a sauce to sugar.

JAQUES [*aside*].

A material fool!

AUDREY

Well, I am not fair; and therefore I pray the gods make
me honest.

TOUCHSTONE

Truly, and to cast away honesty upon a foul slut, were
to put good meat into an unclean dish.

AUDREY

I am not a slut, though I thank the gods I am foul.

TOUCHSTONE

Well, praised be the gods for thy foulness! sluttishness
may come hereafter. But be it as it may be, I will marry
thee: and to that end I have been with Sir Oliver
Martext, the vicar of the next village; who hath promised
to meet me in this place of the forest, and to couple us.

JAQUES [*aside*].

I would fain see this meeting.

AUDREY

Well, the gods give us joy!

TOUCHSTONE

Amen. A man may, if he were of a fearful heart, stagger
in this attempt; for here we have no temple but the
wood, no assembly but horn-beasts. But what though?
Courage! As horns are odious, they are necessary. It is
said, 'Many a man knows no end of his goods': right;
many a man has good horns, and knows no end of
them. Well, that is the dowry of his wife; 'tis none of his
own getting. Horns? even so; poor men alone? No, no;
the noblest deer hath them as huge as the rascal. Is the
single man therefore blessed? No: as a wall'd town is
more worthier than a village, so is the forehead of a
married man more honourable than the bare brow of a
bachelor; and by how much defence is better than no
skill, by so much is a horn more precious than to want.
— Here comes Sir Oliver.

Enter SIR OLIVER MARTEXT.

Sir Oliver Martext, you are well met: will you dispatch
us here under this tree, or shall we go with you to your
chapel?

MARTEXT

Is there none here to give the woman?

TOUCHSTONE

I will not take her on gift of any man.

MARTEXT

Truly, she must be given, or the marriage is not lawful.

JAQUES [*coming forward*].

Proceed, proceed: I'll give her.

TOUCHSTONE

Good even, good Master What-ye-call't: how do you, sir? You are very well met: God ild you for your last company: I am very glad to see you: — even a toy in hand here, sir: — nay, pray be cover'd.

JAQUES

Will you be married, motley?

TOUCHSTONE

As the ox hath his bow, sir, the horse his curb, and the falcon her bells, so man hath his desires; and as pigeons bill, so wedlock would be nibbling.

JAQUES

And will you, being a man of your breeding, be married under a bush like a beggar? Get you to church and have a good priest that can tell you what marriage is: this fellow will but join you together as they join wainscot; then one of you will prove a shrunk panel, and like green timber, warp, warp.

TOUCHSTONE [*aside*].

I am not in the mind but I were better to be married of him than of another: for he is not like to marry me well; and not being well married, it will be a good excuse for me hereafter to leave my wife.

JAQUES

Go thou with me, and let me counsel thee.

TOUCHSTONE

Come, sweet Audrey:

We must be married, or we must live in bawdry. —

Farewell, good Master Oliver: — not,

    O sweet Oliver,

    O brave Oliver,

  Leave me not behind thee; —

but,

    Wind away,

Be gone, I say,
I will not to wedding with thee.
  [*Exeunt* JAQUES, TOUCHSTONE, *and* AUDREY.

MARTEXT
'Tis no matter: ne'er a fantastical knave of them all shall
flout me out of my calling.   [*Exit.*

SCENE IV

The forest.

Enter ROSALIND *and* CELIA.

ROSALIND
Never talk to me; I will weep.

CELIA
Do, I prithee; but yet have the grace to consider that
tears do not become a man.

ROSALIND
But have I not cause to weep?

CELIA
As good cause as one would desire: therefore weep.

ROSALIND
His very hair is of the dissembling colour.

CELIA
Something browner than Judas's: marry, his kisses are
Judas's own children.

ROSALIND
I'faith, his hair is of a good colour.

CELIA
An excellent colour: your chestnut was ever the only
colour.

ROSALIND
And his kissing is as full of sanctity as the touch of holy
bread.

CELIA
He hath bought a pair of cast lips of Diana: a nun of
winter's sisterhood kisses not more religiously; the very
ice of chastity is in them.

ROSALIND

But why did he swear he would come this morning, and comes not?

CELIA

Nay, certainly, there is no truth in him.

ROSALIND

Do you think so?

CELIA

Yes; I think he is not a pick-purse nor a horse-stealer; but for his verity in love, I do think him as concave as a cover'd goblet or a worm-eaten nut.

ROSALIND

Not true in love?

CELIA

Yes, when he is in; but I think he is not in.

ROSALIND

You have heard him swear downright he was.

CELIA

'Was' is not 'is': besides, the oath of a lover is no stronger than the word of a tapster; they are both the confirmers of false reckonings. He attends here in the forest on the duke your father.

ROSALIND

I met the duke yesterday, and had much question with him: he ask'd me, of what parentage I was; I told him, of as good as he; so he laugh'd, and let me go. But what talk we of fathers, when there is such a man as Orlando?

CELIA

O, that's a brave man! he writes brave verses, speaks brave words, swears brave oaths, and breaks them bravely, quite traverse, athwart the heart of his lover; as a puisny tilter, that spurs his horse but on one side, breaks his staff like a noble goose: but all's brave that youth mounts and folly guides. — Who comes here?

Enter CORIN.

CORIN

Mistress and master, you have oft inquired
After the shepherd that complain'd of love,
Who you saw sitting by me on the turf,
Praising the proud disdainful shepherdess
That was his mistress.

CELIA

              Well, and what of him?

CORIN

If you will see a pageant truly play'd,
Between the pale complexion of true love
And the red glow of scorn and proud disdain,
Go hence a little, and I shall conduct you,
If you will mark it.

ROSALIND

           O, come, let us remove:
The sight of lovers feedeth those in love. —
Bring us to this sight, and you shall say
I'll prove a busy actor in their play.   [*Exeunt.*

SCENE V

The forest.

Enter SILVIUS *and* PHEBE.

SILVIUS

Sweet Phebe, do not scorn me; do not, Phebe:
Say that you love me not; but say not so
In bitterness. The common executioner,
Whose heart th'accustom'd sight of death makes hard,
Falls not the axe upon the humbled neck
But first begs pardon: will you sterner be
Than he that dies and lives by bloody drops?

Enter ROSALIND *and* CELIA; CORIN *behind.*

PHEBE

I would not be thy executioner:
I fly thee, for I would not injure thee.

Thou tell'st me there is murder in mine eye:
'Tis pretty, sure, and very probable,
That eyes — that are the frail'st and softest things,
Who shut their coward gates on atomies —
Should be call'd tyrants, butchers, murderers!
Now I do frown on thee with all my heart;
And, if mine eyes can wound, now let them kill thee:
Now counterfeit to swoon; why, now fall down;
Or, if thou canst not, O, for shame, for shame,
Lie not, to say mine eyes are murderers!
Now show the wound mine eye hath made in thee:
Scratch thee but with a pin, and there remains
Some scar of it; lean but upon a rush,
The cicatrice and capable impressure
Thy palm some moment keeps: but now mine eyes,
Which I have darted at thee, hurt thee not;
Nor, I am sure, there is no force in eyes
That can do hurt.

SILVIUS

     O dear Phebe,
If ever — as that ever may be near —
You meet in some fresh cheek the power of fancy,
Then shall you know the wounds invisible
That love's keen arrows make.

PHEBE

        But, till that time,
Come not thou near me: and, when that time comes,
Afflict me with thy mocks, pity me not;
As, till that time, I shall not pity thee.

ROSALIND [coming forward].
And why, I pray you? Who might be your mother,
That you insult, exult, and all at once,
Over the wretched? What though you have no beauty, —
As, by my faith, I see no more in you
Than without candle may go dark to bed, —
Must you be therefore proud and pitiless?
Why, what means this? Why do you look on me?

I see no more in you than in the ordinary
Of nature's sale-work: — 'Od's my little life,
I think she means to tangle my eyes too! —
No, faith, proud mistress, hope not after it:
'Tis not your inky brows, your black-silk hair,
Your bugle eyeballs, nor your cheek of cream,
That can entame my spirits to your worship. —
You foolish shepherd, wherefore do you follow her,
Like foggy south, puffing with wind and rain?
You are a thousand times a properer man
Than she a woman: 'tis such fools as you
That makes the world full of ill-favour'd children:
'Tis not her glass, but you, that flatters her;
And out of you she sees herself more proper
Than any of her lineaments can show her. —
But, mistress, know yourself: down on your knees,
And thank heaven, fasting, for a good man's love:
For I must tell you friendly in your ear, —
Sell when you can: you are not for all markets:
Cry the man mercy; love him; take his offer:
Foul is most foul, being foul to be a scoffer. —
So, take her to thee, shepherd: — fare you well.

PHEBE

Sweet youth, I pray you, chide a year together:
I had rather hear you chide than this man woo.

ROSALIND

He's fall'n in love with her foulness, and she'll fall in
love with my anger: — If it be so, as fast as she answers
thee with frowning looks, I'll sauce her with bitter
words. — Why look you so upon me?

PHEBE

For no ill will I bear you.

ROSALIND

I pray you, do not fall in love with me,
For I am falser than vows made in wine:
Besides, I like you not. — If you will know my
      house,

'Tis at the tuft of olives here hard by. —
Will you go, sister? — Shepherd, ply her hard. —
Come, sister. — Shepherdess, look on him better,
And be not proud: though all the world could see,
None could be so abus'd in sight as he. —
Come, to our flock.

    [*Exeunt* ROSALIND, CELIA, *and* CORIN.

PHEBE
  Dead shepherd, now I find thy saw of might, —
  'Who ever lov'd that lov'd not at first sight?'

SILVIUS
  Sweet Phebe, —

PHEBE
              Ha, what say'st thou, Silvius?

SILVIUS
  Sweet Phebe, pity me.

PHEBE
  Why, I am sorry for thee, gentle Silvius.

SILVIUS
  Wherever sorrow is, relief would be:
  If you do sorrow at my grief in love,
  By giving love, your sorrow and my grief
  Were both extermined.

PHEBE
  Thou hast my love: is not that neighbourly?

SILVIUS
  I would have you.

PHEBE
           Why, that were covetousness.
  Silvius, the time was, that I hated thee;
  And yet it is not that I bear thee love:
  But since that thou canst talk of love so well,
  Thy company, which erst was irksome to me,
  I will endure; and I'll employ thee too:
  But do not look for further recompense
  Than thine own gladness that thou art employ'd.

SILVIUS
  So holy and so perfect is my love,
  And I in such a poverty of grace,
  That I shall think it a most plenteous crop
  To glean the broken ears after the man
  That the main harvest reaps: loose now and then
  A scatter'd smile, and that I'll live upon.

PHEBE
  Know'st thuo the youth that spoke to me erewhile?

SILVIUS
  Not very well, but I have met him oft;
  And he hath bought the cottage and the bounds
  That the old carlot once was master of.

PHEBE
  Think not I love him, though I ask for him;
  'Tis but a peevish boy: — yet he talks well; —
  But what care I for words? yet words do well,
  When he that speaks them pleases those that hear.
  It is a pretty youth: — not very pretty: —
  But, sure, he's proud; and yet his pride becomes him:
  He'll make a proper man: the best thing in him
  Is his complexion; and faster than his tongue
  Did make offence, his eye did heal it up.
  He is not very tall; yet for his years he's tall:
  His leg is but so-so; and yet 'tis well:
  There was a pretty redness in his lip,
  A little riper and more lusty red
  Than that mix'd in his cheek; 'twas just the difference
  Betwixt the constant red and mingled damask.
  There be some women, Silvius, had they mark'd him
  In parcels as I did, would have gone near
  To fall in love with him: but, for my part,
  I love him not, nor hate him not; and yet
  I have more cause to hate him than to love him:
  For what had he to do to chide at me?
  He said mine eyes were black, and my hair black;
  And, now I am remember'd, scorn'd at me:

I marvel why I answer'd not again:
But that's all one; omittance is no quittance.
I'll write to him a very taunting letter,
And thou shalt bear it; wilt thou, Silvius?

SILVIUS

Phebe, with all my heart.

PHEBE

               I'll write it straight;
The matter's in my head and in my heart:
I will be bitter with him and passing short.
Go with me, Silvius.   [*Exeunt.*

ACT IV

SCENE I

The forest.

Enter ROSALIND, CELIA, *and* JAQUES.

JAQUES

I prithee, pretty youth, let me be better acquainted with
thee.

ROSALIND

They say you are a melancholy fellow.

JAQUES

I am so; I do love it better than laughing.

ROSALIND

Those that are in extremity of either are abominable
fellows, and betray themselves to every modern censure
worse than drunkards.

JAQUES

Why, 'tis good to be sad and say nothing.

ROSALIND

Why, then 'tis good to be a post.

JAQUES

I have neither the scholar's melancholy, which is
emulation; nor the musician's, which is fantastical; nor

the courtier's, which is proud; nor the soldier's, which is
ambitious; nor the lawyer's, which is politic; nor the
lady's, which is nice; nor the lover's, which is all these;
— but it is a melancholy of mine own, compounded of
many simples, extracted from many objects, and,
indeed, the sundry contemplation of my travels, which,
by often rumination, wraps me in a most humorous
sadness.

ROSALIND

A traveller! By my faith, you have great reason to be sad:
I fear you have sold your own lands, to see other men's;
then, to have seen much, and to have nothing, is to have
rich eyes and poor hands.

JAQUES

Yes, I have gain'd my experience.

ROSALIND

And your experience makes you sad: I had rather have a
fool to make me merry than experience to make me sad;
and to travel for it too!

Enter ORLANDO.

ORLANDO

Good day and happiness, dear Rosalind!

JAQUES

Nay, then, God b'wi'you, an you talk in blank verse!

[*Exit.*

ROSALIND

Farewell, Monsieur Traveller: look you lisp, and wear
strange suits; disable all the benefits of your own
country; be out of love with your nativity, and almost
chide God for making you that countenance you are; or
I will scarce think you have swam in a gondola. Why,
how now, Orlando! where have you been all this while?
You a lover! — An you serve me such another trick,
never come in my sight more.

ORLANDO

My fair Rosalind, I come within an hour of my promise.

ROSALIND

Break an hour's promise in love! He that will divide a
minute into a thousand parts, and break but a part of
the thousandth part of a minute in the affairs of love, it
may be said of him, that Cupid hath clapp'd him
o'th'shoulder, but I'll warrant him heart-whole.

ORLANDO

Pardon me, dear Rosalind.

ROSALIND

Nay, an you be so tardy, come no more in my sight: had
as lief be woo'd of a snail.

ORLANDO

Of a snail!

ROSALIND

Ay, of a snail; for though he comes slowly, he carries his
house on his head, — a better jointure, I think, than you
make a woman: besides, he brings his destiny with him.

ORLANDO

What's that?

ROSALIND

Why, horns; which such as you are fain to be beholding
to your wives for: but he comes arm'd in his fortune,
and prevents the slander of his wife.

ORLANDO

Virtue is no horn-maker; and my Rosalind is virtuous.

ROSALIND

And I am your Rosalind.

CELIA

It pleases him to call you so; but he hath a Rosalind of a
better leer than you.

ROSALIND

Come, woo me, woo me; for now I am in a holiday
humour, and like enough to consent. — What would
you say to me now, an I were your very very Rosalind?

ORLANDO

I would kiss before I spoke.

ROSALIND

Nay, you were better speak first; and when you were
gravell'd for lack of matter, you might take occasion to
kiss. Very good orators, when they are out, they will spit;
and for lovers, lacking (God warn us!) matter, the
cleanliest shift is to kiss.

ORLANDO

How if the kiss be denied?

ROSALIND

Then she puts you to entreaty, and there begins new
matter.

ORLANDO

Who could be out, being before his beloved mistress?

ROSALIND

Marry, that should you, if I were your mistress; or I
should think my honesty ranker than my wit.

ORLANDO

What, of my suit?

ROSALIND

Not out of your apparel, and yet out of your suit.
Am not I your Rosalind?

ORLANDO

I take some joy to say you are, because I would be
talking of her.

ROSALIND

Well, in her person, I say, — I will not have you.

ORLANDO

Then, in mine own person, I die.

ROSALIND

No, faith, die by attorney. The poor world is almost six
thousand years old, and in all this time there was not
any man died in his own person, *videlicet*, in a love-
cause. Troilus had his brains dash'd out with a Grecian
club; yet he did what he could to die before; and he is
one of the patterns of love. Leander, he would have
lived many a fair year, though Hero had turn'd nun, if it

had not been for a hot midsummer night; for, good youth, he went but forth to wash him in the Hellespont, and, being taken with the cramp, was drown'd: and the foolish chroniclers of that age found it was — Hero of Sestos. But these are all lies: men have died from time to time, and worms have eaten them, but not for love.

ORLANDO
I would not have my right Rosalind of this mind; for, I protest, her frown might kill me.

ROSALIND
By this hand, it will not kill a fly. But come, now I will be your Rosalind in a more coming-on disposition; and ask me what you will, I will grant it.

ORLANDO
Then love me, Rosalind.

ROSALIND
Yes, faith, will I, Fridays and Saturdays and all.

ORLANDO
And wilt thou have me?

ROSALIND
Ay, and twenty such.

ORLANDO
What sayest thou?

ROSALIND
Are you not good?

ORLANDO
I hope so.

ROSALIND
Why, then, can one desire too much of a good thing? — Come, sister, you shall be the priest, and marry us. — Give me your hand, Orlando. — What do you say, sister?

ORLANDO
Pray thee, marry us.

CELIA
I cannot say the words.

ROSALIND

You must begin, — 'Will you, Orlando,' —

CELIA

Go to. — Will you, Orlando, have to wife this Rosalind?

ORLANDO

I will.

ROSALIND

Ay, but when?

ORLANDO

Why now; as fast as she can marry us.

ROSALIND

Then you must say, — 'I take thee, Rosalind, for wife.'

ORLANDO

I take thee, Rosalind, for wife.

ORLANDO I take thee, Rosalind, for wife.

ROSALIND

I might ask you for your commission; but, — I do take thee, Orlando, for my husband: — there's a girl goes before the priest; and, certainly, a woman's thought runs before her actions.

ORLANDO

So do all thoughts, — they are wing'd.

ROSALIND

Now tell me how long you would have her, after you have possess'd her.

ORLANDO

For ever and a day.

ROSALIND

Say a day, without the ever. No, no, Orlando; men are April when they woo, December when they wed: maids are May when they are maids, but the sky changes when they are wives. I will be more jealous of thee than a Barbary cock-pigeon over his hen; more clamorous than a parrot against rain; more new-fangled than an ape; more giddy in my desires than a monkey: I will weep for nothing, like Diana in the fountain, and I will do that when you are disposed to be merry; I will laugh like a hyen, and that when thou art inclined towleep.

ORLANDO

But will my Rosalind do so?

ROSALIND

By my life, she will do as I do.

ORLANDO

O, but she is wise.

ROSALIND

Or else she could not have the wit to do this: the wiser, the waywarder: make the doors upon a woman's wit, and it will out at the casement; shut that, and 'twill out at the key-hole; stop that, 'twill fly with the smoke out at the chimney.

ORLANDO

A man that had a wife with such a wit, he might say, — 'Wit, whither wilt?'

ROSALIND

Nay, you might keep that check for it till you met your wife's wit going to your neighbour's bed.

ORLANDO

And what wit could wit have to excuse that?

ROSALIND

Marry, to say, — she came to seek you there. You shall never take her without her answer, unless you take her without her tongue. O, that woman that cannot make her fault her husband's occasion, let her never nurse her child herself, for she will breed it like a fool!

ORLANDO

For these two hours, Rosalind, I will leave thee.

ROSALIND

Alas! dear love, I cannot lack thee two hours!

ORLANDO

I must attend the duke at dinner: by two o'clock I will be with thee again.

ROSALIND

Ay, go your ways, go your ways; — I knew what you would prove: my friends told me as much, and I thought no less: — that flattering tongue of yours won me: — 'tis but one cast away, and so, — come, death! — Two o'clock is your hour?

ORLANDO

Ay, sweet Rosalind.

ROSALIND

By my troth, and in good earnest, and so God mend me, and by all pretty oaths that are not dangerous, if you break one jot of your promise, or come one minute behind your hour, I will think you the most pathetical break-promise, and the most hollow lover, and the most unworthy of her you call Rosalind, that may be chosen out of the gross band of the unfaithful: therefore beware my censure, and keep your promise.

ORLANDO

With no less religion than if thou wert indeed my Rosalind: so, adieu.

81

ROSALIND

Well, Time is the old justice that examines all such offenders, and let Time try: adieu. [*Exit* ORLANDO.

CELIA

You have simply misused our sex in your love-prate: we must have your doublet and hose pluck'd over your head, and show the world what the bird hath done to her own nest.

ROSALIND

O coz, coz, coz, my pretty little coz, that thou didst know how many fathom deep I am in love! But it cannot be sounded: my affection hath an unknown bottom, like the bay of Portugal.

CELIA

Or rather, bottomless; that as fast as you pour affection in, it runs out.

ROSALIND

No, that same wicked bastard of Venus, that was begot of thought, conceived of spleen, and born of madness; that blind rascally boy, that abuses every one's eyes, because his own are out, let him be judge how deep I am in love: — I'll tell thee, Aliena, I cannot be out of the sight of Orlando; I'll go find a shadow, and sigh till he come.

CELIA

And I'll sleep. [*Exeunt.*

SCENE II

The forest.

Enter JAQUES, LORDS, *and* FORESTERS.

JAQUES

Which is he that kill'd the deer?

A LORD

Sir, it was I.

JAQUES

Let's present him to the duke, like a Roman conqueror; and it would do well to set the deer's horns upon his

head, for a branch of victory. — Have you no song,
forester, for this purpose?

FORESTER

Yes, sir.

JAQUES

Sing it: 'tis no matter how it be in tune, so it make noise
enough.

Song.

What shall he have that kill'd the deer?
His leather skin and horns to wear.
Then sing him home!
[*The rest shall bear this burthen.*
Take thou no scorn to wear the horn;
It was a crest ere thou wast born;
Thy father's father wore it,
And thy father bore it:
The horn, the horn, the lusty horn
Is not a thing to laugh to scorn. [*Exeunt.*

SCENE III

The forest.

Enter ROSALIND *and* CELIA.

ROSALIND

How say you now? Is it not past two o'clock? and here
much Orlando!

CELIA

I warrant you, with pure love and troubled brain, he
hath ta'en his bow and arrows, and is gone forth — to
sleep. Look, who comes here.

Enter SILVIUS.

SILVIUS

My errand is to you, fair youth; —
My gentle Phebe bid me give you this:
[*Gives a letter.*

I know not the contents; but, as I guess
By the stern brow and waspish action
Which she did use as she was writing of it,
It bears an angry tenor: pardon me,
I am but as a guiltless messenger.

ROSALIND

Patience herself would startle at this letter,
And play the swaggerer; bear this, bear all:
She says I am not fair; that I lack manners;
She calls me proud; and that she could not love me,
Were man as rare as phœnix. 'Od's my will!
Her love is not the hare that I do hunt:
Why writes she so to me? — Well, shepherd, well,
This is a letter of your own device.

SILVIUS

No, I protest, I know not the contents:
Phebe did write it.

ROSALIND

            Come, come, you are a fool,
And turn'd into the extremity of love.
I saw her hand: she has a leathern hand,
A freestone-colour'd hand; I verily did think
That her old gloves were on, but 'twas her hands:
She has a housewife's hand; but that's no matter:
I say, she never did invent this letter;
This is a man's invention, and his hand.

SILVIUS

Sure, it is hers.

ROSALIND

Why, 'tis a boisterous and a cruel style,
A style for challengers: why, she defies me,
Like Turk to Christian: women's gentle brain
Could not drop forth such giant-rude invention,
Such Ethiop words, blacker in their effect
Than in their countenance. — Will you hear me letter?

SILVIUS

So please you, for I never heard it yet;

Yet heard too much of Phebe's cruelty.

ROSALIND
  She Phebes me: mark how the tyrant writes.
  [*Reads*] Art thou god to shepherd turn'd,
        That a maiden's heart hath burn'd? —
  Can a woman rail thus?

SILVIUS
  Call you this railing?

ROSALIND [*reads*].
        Why, thy godhead laid apart,
        Warr'st thou with a woman's heart? —
  Did you ever hear such railing? —
        Whiles the eye of man did woo me,
        That could do no vengeance to me. —
  Meaning me a beast. —
        If the scorn of your bright eyne
        Have power to raise such love in mine,
        Alack, in me what strange effect
        Would they work in mild aspect!
        Whiles you chid me, I did love;
        How, then, might your prayers move!
        He that brings this love to thee
        Little knows this love in me:
        And by him seal up thy mind;
        Whether that thy youth and kind
        Will the faithful offer take
        Of me, and all that I can make;
        Or else by him my love deny,
        And then I'll study how to die.

SILVIUS
  Call you this chiding?

CELIA
  Alas, poor shepherd!

ROSALIND
  Do you pity him? no, he deserves no pity. Wilt thou love
  such a woman? What, to make thee an instrument, and
  play false strains upon thee! not to be endured! Well, go

85

your way to her, for I see love hath made thee a tame
snake, and say this to her: — that if she love me, I charge
her to love thee; if she will not, I will never have her, unless
thou entreat for her. — If you be a true lover, hence, and
not a word; for here comes more company.

[*Exit* SILVIUS.

Enter OLIVER.

OLIVER
  Good morrow, fair ones: pray you, if you know,
  Where in the purlieus of this forest stands
  A sheep-cote fenc'd about with olive-trees?

CELIA
  West of this place, down in the neighbour bottom:
  The rank of osiers, by the murmuring stream,
  Left on your right hand, brings you to the place.
  But at this hour the house doth keep itself;
  There's none within.

OLIVER
  If that an eye may profit by a tongue,
  Then should I know you by description;
  Such garments and such years: — 'The boy is fair,
  Of female favour, and bestows himself
  Like a ripe sister: the woman low,
  And browner than her brother.' Are not you
  The owners of the house I did inquire for?

CELIA
  It is no boast, being ask'd, to say we are.

OLIVER
  Orlando doth commend him to you both;
  And to that youth he calls his Rosalind
  He sends this bloody napkin; — are you he?

ROSALIND
  I am: what must we understand by this?

OLIVER
  Some of my shame; if you will know of me
  What man I am, and how, and why, and where

86

This handkercher was stain'd.

CELIA

I pray you, tell it.

OLIVER

When last the young Orlando parted from you,
He left a promise to return again
Within an hour; and, pacing through the forest,
Chewing the food of sweet and bitter fancy,
Lo, what befell! he threw his eye aside,
And, mark, what object did present itself:
Under an oak, whose boughs were moss'd with age,
And high top bald with dry antiquity,
A wretched ragged man, o'ergrown with hair,
Lay sleeping on his back: about his neck
A green and gilded snake had wreath'd itself,
Who with her head, nimble in threats, approach'd
The opening of his mouth; but suddenly,
Seeing Orlando, it unlink'd itself,
And with indented glides did slip away
Into a bush: under which bush's shade
A lioness, with udders all drawn dry,
Lay couching, head on ground, with catlike watch,
When that the sleeping man should stir; for 'tis
The royal disposition of that beast
To prey on nothing that doth seem as dead:
This seen, Orlando did approach the man,
And found it was his brother, his elder brother.

CELIA

O, I have heard him speak of that same brother;
And he did render him the most unnatural
That liv'd 'mongst men.

OLIVER

And well he might so do,
For well I know he was unnatural.

ROSALIND

But, to Orlando: — did he leave him there,
Food to the suck'd and hungry lioness?

OLIVER
  Twice did he turn his back, and purpos'd so;
  But kindness, nobler ever than revenge,
  And nature, stronger than his just occasion,
  Made him give battle to the lioness,
  Who quickly fell before him: in which hurtling
  From miserable slumber I awak'd.

CELIA
  Are you his brother?

ROSALIND
                    Was't you he rescued?

CELIA
  Was't you that did so oft contrive to kill him?

OLIVER
  'Twas I: but 'tis not I: I do not shame
  To tell you what I was, since my conversion
  So sweetly tastes, being the thing I am.

ROSALIND
  But, for the bloody napkin? —

OLIVER
                          By and by.
  When from the first to last, betwixt us two,
  Tears our recountments had most kindly bathed,
  As how I came into that desert place; —
  In brief, he led me to the gentle duke,
  Who gave me fresh array and entertainment,
  Committing me unto my brother's love;
  Who led me instantly unto his cave,
  There stripp'd himself, and here upon his arm
  The lioness had torn some flesh away,
  Which all this while had bled; and now he fainted
  And cried, in fainting, upon Rosalind.
  Brief, I recover'd him, bound up his wound;
  And, after some small space, being strong at heart,
  He sent me hither, stranger as I am,
  To tell this story, that you might excuse
  His broken promise, and to give this napkin,

Dyed in his blood, unto the shepherd youth
That he in sport doth call his Rosalind.

CELIA

Why, how now, Ganymede! sweet Ganymede!

[ROSALIND *faints.*

OLIVER

Many will swoon when they do look on blood.

CELIA

There is more in it. — Cousin Ganymede!

OLIVER

Look, he recovers.

ROSALIND

I would I were at home.

CELIA

We'll lead you thither. —
I pray you, will you take him by the arm?

OLIVER

Be of good cheer, youth: — you a man? you lack a
man's heart.

ROSALIND

I do so, I confess it! Ah, sirrah, a body would think this
was well counterfeited! I pray you, tell your brother how
well I counterfeited. — Heigh-ho!

OLIVER

This was not counterfeit: there is too great testimony in
your complexion, that it was a passion of earnest.

ROSALIND

Counterfeit, I assure you.

OLIVER

Well, then, take a good heart, and counterfeit to be a man.

ROSALIND

So I do: but, i'faith, I should have been a woman by
right.

CELIA

Come, you look paler and paler: pray you, draw
homewards. — Good sir, go with us.

OLIVER
That will I, for I must bear answer back
How you excuse my brother, Rosalind.

ROSALIND
I shall devise something: but, I pray you, commend my
counterfeiting to him: — Will you go?   [*Exeunt.*

ACT V

SCENE I

The forest.
Enter TOUCHSTONE *and* AUDREY.

TOUCHSTONE
We shall find a time, Audrey; patience, gentle Audrey.

AUDREY
Faith, the priest was good enough, for all the old
gentleman's saying.

TOUCHSTONE
A most wicked Sir Oliver, Audrey, a most vile Martext.
But, Audrey, there is a youth here in the forest lays
claim to you.

AUDREY
Ay, I know who 'tis; he hath no interest in me in the
world: here comes the man you mean.

TOUCHSTONE
It is meat and drink to me to see a clown: by my troth,
we that have good wits have much to answer for; we
shall be flouting; we cannot hold.

Enter WILLIAM.

WILLIAM
Good even, Audrey.

AUDREY
God ye good even, William.

WILLIAM
And good even to you, sir.

TOUCHSTONE
  Good even, gentle friend. Cover thy head, cover thy
  head: nay, prithee, be cover'd. How old are you, friend?

WILLIAM
  Five and twenty, sir.

TOUCHSTONE
  A ripe age. Is thy name William?

WILLIAM
  William, sir.

TOUCHSTONE
  A fair name. Wast born i'th'forest here?

WILLIAM
  Ay, sir, I thank God.

TOUCHSTONE
  Thank God; — a good answer. Art rich?

WILLIAM
  Faith, sir, so-so.

TOUCHSTONE
  So-so is good, very good, very excellent good: — and yet
  it is not; it is but so-so. Art thou wise?

WILLIAM
  Ay, sir, I have a pretty wit.

TOUCHSTONE
  Why, thou say'st well. I do now remember a saying,
  'The fool doth think he is wise; but the wise man knows
  himself to be a fool.' The heathen philosopher, when he
  had a desire to eat a grape, would open his lips when he
  put it into his mouth; meaning thereby, that grapes were
  made to eat, and lips to open. You do love this maid?

WILLIAM
  I do, sir.

TOUCHSTONE
  Give me your hand. Art thou learned?

WILLIAM
  No, sir.

TOUCHSTONE

Then learn this of me: — to have, is to have; for it is a
figure in rhetoric, that drink, being pour'd out of a cup
into a glass, by filling the one doth empty the other; for
all your writers do consent that *ipse* is he: now, you are
not *ipse*, for I am he.

WILLIAM

Which he, sir?

TOUCHSTONE

He, sir, that must marry this woman. Therefore, you
clown, abandon, — which is in the vulgar leave, — the
society, — which in the boorish is company, — of this
female, — which in the common is woman; which
together is, abandon the society of this female, or,
clown, thou perishest; or, to thy better understanding,

TOUCHSTONE Therefore, you clown, abandon.

diest; or (to wit) I kill thee, make thee away, translate
thy life into death, thy liberty into bondage: I will deal
in poison with thee, or in bastinado, or in steel; I will
bandy with thee in faction; I will o'er-run thee with
policy; I will kill thee a hundred and fifty ways:
therefore tremble, and depart.

AUDREY

Do, good William.

WILLIAM

God rest you merry, sir.   [Exit.

                    Enter CORIN.

CORIN

Our master and mistress seek you; come, away, away!

TOUCHSTONE

Trip, Audrey, trip, Audrey. — I attend, I attend.[Exeunt.

SCENE II

The forest.

Enter ORLANDO *and* OLIVER.

ORLANDO

Is't possible that, on so little acquaintance, you should
like her? that, but seeing, you should love her? and,
loving, woo? and, wooing, she should grant? and will
you persever to enjoy her?

OLIVER

Neither call the giddiness of it in question, the poverty
of her, the small acquaintance, my sudden wooing, nor
her sudden consenting; but say with me, I love Aliena;
say with her, that she loves me; consent with both, that
we may enjoy each other: it shall be to your good; for
my father's house, and all the revenue that was old Sir
Rowland's, will I estate upon you, and here live and die
a shepherd.

ORLANDO

You have my consent. Let your wedding be to-morrow:
thither will I invite the duke, and all's contented
followers. Go you and prepare Aliena; for, look you,
here comes my Rosalind.

Enter ROSALIND.

ROSALIND

God save you, brother.

OLIVER

And you, fair sister.   [*Exit.*

ROSALIND

O, my dear Orlando, how it grieves me to see thee wear
thy heart in a scarf!

ORLANDO

It is my arm.

ROSALIND

I thought thy heart had been wounded with the claws of
a lion.

ORLANDO

Wounded it is, but with the eyes of a lady.

ROSALIND

Did your brother tell you how I counterfeited to swoon
when he show'd me your handkercher?

ORLANDO

Ay, and greater wonders than that.

ROSALIND

O, I know where you are: — nay, 'tis true: there was
never any thing so sudden, but the fight of two rams,
and Cæsar's thrasonical brag of — 'I came, saw, and
overcame': for your brother and my sister no sooner
met, but they look'd; no sooner look'd, but they loved;
no sooner loved, but they sigh'd; no sooner sigh'd, but
they ask'd one another the reason; no sooner knew the
reason, but they sought the remedy: and in these degrees
have they made a pair of stairs to marriage, which they
will climb incontinent, or else be incontinent before

marriage: they are in the very wrath of love, and they will together; clubs cannot part them.

ORLANDO

They shall be married to-morrow; and I will bid the duke to the nuptial. But, O, how bitter a thing it is to look into happiness through another man's eyes! By so much the more shall I to-morrow be at the height of heart-heaviness, by how much I shall think my brother happy in having what he wishes for.

ROSALIND

Why, then, to-morrow I cannot serve your turn for Rosalind?

ORLANDO

I can live no longer by thinking.

ROSALIND

I will weary you, then, no longer with idle talking. Know of me, then — for now I speak to some purpose, — that I know you are a gentleman of good conceit: I speak not this, that you should bear a good opinion of my knowledge, insomuch I say I know you are; neither do I labour for a greater esteem than may in some little measure draw a belief from you, to do yourself good, and not to grace me. Believe, then, if you please, that I can do strange things: I have, since I was three year old, conversed with a magician, most profound in his art, and yet not damnable. If you do love Rosalind so near the heart as your gesture cries it out, when your brother marries Aliena, shall you marry her: I know into what straits of fortune she is driven; and it is not impossible to me, if it appear not inconvenient to you, to set her before your eyes to-morrow human as she is, and without any danger.

ORLANDO

Speak'st thou in sober meanings?

ROSALIND

By my life I do; which I tender dearly, though I say I am a magician. Therefore, put you in your best array, bid

your friends; for if you will be married to-morrow, you
shall; and to Rosalind, if you will. — Look, here comes a
lover of mine, and a lover of hers.

Enter SILVIUS *and* PHEBE.

PHEBE

Youth, you have done me much ungentleness,
To show the letter that I writ to you.

ROSALIND

I care not, if I have: it is my study
To seem despiteful and ungentle to you:
You are there follow'd by a faithful shepherd;
Look upon him, love him; he worships you.

PHEBE

Good shepherd, tell this youth what 'tis to love.

SILVIUS

It is to be all made of sighs and tears; —
And so am I for Phebe.

PHEBE

And I for Ganymede.

ORLANDO

And I for Rosalind.

ROSALIND

And I for no woman.

SILVIUS

It is to be all made of faith and service; —
And so am I for Phebe.

PHEBE

And I for Ganymede.

ORLANDO

And I for Rosalind.

ROSALIND

And I for no woman.

SILVIUS

It is to be all made of fantasy,
All made of passion, and all made of wishes;
All adoration, duty, and observance,

All humbleness, all patience, and impatience,
All purity, all trial, all deservings; —
And so am I for Phebe.

PHEBE
  And so am I for Ganymede.

ORLANDO
  And so am I for Rosalind.

ROSALIND
  And so am I for no woman.

PHEBE [*to* ROSALIND].
  If this be so, why blame you me to love you?

SILVIUS [*to* PHEBE].
  If this be so, why blame you me to love you?

ORLANDO
  If this be so, why blame you me to love you?

ROSALIND
  Who do you speak to, — 'Why blame you me to love
  you?'

ORLANDO
  To her that is not here, nor doth not hear.

ROSALIND
  Pray you, no more of this; 'tis like the howling of Irish
  wolves against the moon. — I will help you [*to*
  SILVIUS], if I can: — I would love you [*to* PHEBE], if I
  could. — To-morrow meet me all together. — I will
  marry you [*to* PHEBE], if ever I marry woman, and I'll
  be married to-morrow; — I will satisfy you [*to*
  ORLANDO], if ever I satisfy man, and you shall be
  married to-morrow: — I will content you [*to* SILVIUS],
  if what pleases you contents you, and you shall be
  married to-morrow. — As you [*to* ORLANDO] love
  Rosalind, meet: — as you [*to* SILVIUS] love Phebe,
  meet: and as I love no woman, I'll meet. — So, fare you
  well: I have left you commands.

SILVIUS
  I'll not fail, if I live.

PHEBE
  Nor I.

ORLANDO
  Nor I.   [*Exeunt.*

SCENE III

The forest.

Enter TOUCHSTONE *and* AUDREY.

TOUCHSTONE
  To-morrow is the joyful day, Audrey; to-morrow will we
  be married.

AUDREY
  I do desire it with all my heart; and I hope it is no
  dishonest desire, to desire to be a woman of the world.
  Here come two of the banish'd duke's pages.

Enter two PAGES.

FIRST PAGE
  Well met, honest gentleman.

TOUCHSTONE
  By my troth, well met. Come, sit, sit, and a song.

SECOND PAGE
  We are for you: sit i'th'middle.

FIRST PAGE
  Shall we clap into't roundly, without hawking, or
  spitting, or saying we are hoarse, which are the only
  prologues to a bad voice?

SECOND PAGE
  I'faith, i'faith; and both in a tune, like two gipsies on a
  horse.

  Song.

      It was a lover and his lass,
          With a hey, and a ho, and a hey nonino,
     That o'er the green corn-field did pass
          In spring-time, the only pretty ring-time,

When birds do sing, hey ding a ding, ding:
Sweet lovers love the spring.
Between the acres of the rye,
    With a hey, and a ho, and a hey nonino,
These pretty country-folks would lie
    In spring-time, *etc.*
This carol they began that hour,
    With a hey, and a ho, and a hey nonino,
How that a life was but a flower
    In spring-time, *etc.*
And therefore take the present time,
    With a hey, and a ho, and a hey nonino;
For love is crowned with the prime
    In spring time, *etc.*

TOUCHSTONE
  Truly, young gentlemen, though there was no great
  matter in the ditty, yet the note was very untuneable.

FIRST PAGE
  You are deceived, sir: we kept time, we lost not our
  time.

TOUCHSTONE
  By my troth, yes; I count it but time lost to hear such a
  foolish song. God b' wi' you; and God mend your voices!
  — Come, Audrey.   [*Exeunt.*

SCENE IV

The forest.

Enter DUKE SENIOR, AMIENS, JAQUES,
ORLANDO, OLIVER, *and* CELIA.

DUKE SENIOR
  Dost thou believe, Orlando, that the boy
  Can do all this that he hath promised?

ORLANDO
  I sometimes do believe, and sometimes do not;
  As those that fear, — they hope, and know they fear.

Enter ROSALIND, SILVIUS, *and* PHEBE.

ROSALIND
  Patience once more, whiles our compact is urged; —
  You say, if I bring in your Rosalind,

  [*To the* DUKE.

  You will bestow her on Orlando here?

DUKE SENIOR
  That would I, had I kingdoms to give with her.

ROSALIND [*to* ORLANDO].
  And you say, you will have her, when I bring her?

ORLANDO
  That would I, were I of all kingdoms king.

ROSALIND [*to* PHEBE].
  You say, you'll marry me, if I be willing?

PHEBE
  That will I, should I die the hour after.

ROSALIND
  But if you do refuse to marry me,
  You'll give yourself to this most faithful shepherd?

PHEBE
  So is the bargain.

ROSALIND [*to* SILVIUS].
  You say, that you'll have Phebe, if she will?

SILVIUS
  Though to have her and death were both one thing.

ROSALIND
  I have promised to make all this matter even.
  Keep you your word, O duke, to give your daughter; —
  You yours, Orlando, to receive his daughter: —
  Keep your word, Phebe, that you'll marry me,
  Or else, refusing me, to wed this shepherd: —
  Keep your word, Silvius, that you'll marry her,
  If she refuse me: — and from hence I go,
  To make these doubts all even.

  [*Exeunt* ROSALIND *and* CELIA.

DUKE SENIOR
  I do remember in this shepherd boy
  Some lively touches of my daughter's favour.

ORLANDO
  My lord, the first time that I ever saw him
  Methought he was a brother to your daughter:
  But, my good lord, this boy is forest-born,
  And hath been tutor'd in the rudiments
  Of many desperate studies by his uncle,
  Whom he reports to be a great magician,
  Obscured in the circle of this forest.

JAQUES
  There is, sure, another flood toward, and these couples
  are coming to the ark. Here comes a pair of very strange
  beasts, which in all tongues are call'd fools.

        Enter TOUCHSTONE and AUDREY.

TOUCHSTONE
  Salutation and greeting to you all!

JAQUES
  Good my lord, bid him welcome: this is the motley-
  minded gentleman that I have so often met in the forest:
  he hath been a courtier, he swears.

TOUCHSTONE
  If any man doubt that, let him put me to my purgation.
  I have trod a measure; I have flatter'd a lady; I have
  been politic with my friend, smooth with mine enemy; I
  have undone three tailors; I have had four quarrels, and
  like to have fought one.

JAQUES
  And how was that ta'en up?

TOUCHSTONE
  Faith, we met, and found the quarrel was upon the
  seventh cause.

JAQUES
  How seventh cause? — Good my lord, like this fellow.

DUKE SENIOR

I like him very well.

TOUCHSTONE

God ild you, sir; I desire you of the like. I press in here, sir, amongst the rest of the country copulatives, to swear and to forswear; according as marriage binds and blood breaks: — a poor virgin, sir, an ill-favour'd thing, sir, but mine own; a poor humour of mine, sir, to take that that no man else will: rich honesty dwells like a miser, sir, in a poor house; as your pearl in your foul oyster.

DUKE SENIOR

By my faith, he is very swift and sententious.

TOUCHSTONE

According to the fool's bolt, sir, and such dulcet diseases.

JAQUES

But, for the seventh cause; how did you find the quarrel on the seventh cause?

TOUCHSTONE

Upon a lie seven times removed: — bear your body more seeming, Audrey: — as thus, sir: I did dislike the cut of a certain courtier's beard: he sent me word, if I said his beard was not cut well, he was in the mind it was: this is call'd the Retort Courteous. If I sent him word again it was not well cut, he would send me word he cut it to please himself: this is call'd the Quip Modest. If again it was not well cut, he disabled my judgement: this is call'd the Reply Churlish. If again it was not well cut, he would answer I spake not true: this is call'd the Reproof Valiant. If again it was not well cut, he would say I lie: this is call'd the Counter-check Quarrelsome: and so to the Lie Circumstantial and the Lie Direct.

JAQUES

And how oft did you say his beard was not well cut?

TOUCHSTONE

I durst go no further than the Lie Circumstantial, nor he durst not give me the Lie Direct; and so we measured swords, and parted.

JAQUES
  Can you nominate in order now the degrees of the lie?

TOUCHSTONE
  O sir, we quarrel in print, by the book; as you have
  books for good manners: I will name you the degrees.
  The first, the Retort Courteous; the second, the Quip
  Modest; the third, the Reply Churlish; the fourth, the
  Reproof Valiant; the fifth, the Countercheck
  Quarrelsome; the sixth, the Lie with Circumstance; the
  seventh, the Lie Direct. All these you may avoid, but the
  Lie Direct; and you may avoid that too with an 'if'. I
  knew when seven justices could not take up a quarrel;
  but when the parties were met themselves, one of them
  thought but of an 'if', as, 'If you said so, then I said so';
  and they shook hands, and swore brothers. Your 'if' is
  the only peacemaker; much virtue in 'if'.

JAQUES
  Is not this a rare fellow, my lord? he's as good at any
  thing, and yet a fool.

DUKE SENIOR
  He uses his folly like a stalking-horse, and under
  the presentation of that he shoots his wit.

  Enter HYMEN *leading* ROSALIND *in woman's clothes,
  and* CELIA.

  Still music.

HYMEN
        Then is there mirth in heaven,
        When earthly things made even
            Atone together.
        Good duke, receive thy daughter:
        Hymen from heaven brought her,
            Yea, brought her hither,
        That thou mightst join her hand with his
        Whose heart within his bosom is.

ROSALIND [*to* DUKE SENIOR].
  To you I give myself, for I am yours. —
  [*to* ORLANDO] To you I give myself, for I am yours.

103

DUKE SENIOR
  If there be truth in sight, you are my daughter.
ORLANDO
  If there be truth in sight, you are my Rosalind.
PHEBE
  If sight and shape be true,
  Why, then, — my love adieu!
ROSALIND [*to* DUKE SENIOR].
  I'll have no father, if you be not he: —
  [*to* ORLANDO] I'll have no husband, if you be not he: —
  [*to* PHEBE] Nor ne'er wed woman, if you be not she.
HYMEN
      Peace, ho! I bar confusion:
      'Tis I must make conclusion
          Of these most strange events:
      Here's eight that must take hands
      To join in Hymen's bands,
          If truth holds true contents.
      You and you no cross shall part: —
              [*To* ORLANDO *and* ROSALIND.
      You and you are heart in heart: —
                  [*To* OLIVER *and* CELIA.
      You to his love must accord,   [*To* PHEBE.
      Or have a woman to your lord: —
      You and you are sure together,
              [*To* TOUCHSTONE *and* AUDREY.
      As the winter to foul weather.
      Whiles a wedlock-hymn we sing,
      Feed yourselves with questioning;
      That reason wonder may diminish,
      How thus we met, and these things finish.
    Song.
      Wedding is great Juno's crown:
          O blessed bond of board and bed!
      'Tis Hymen peoples every town;
          High wedlock, then, be honoured:
      Honour, high honour, and renown,

     To Hymen, god of every town!

DUKE SENIOR
  O my dear niece, welcome thou art to me,
  Even daughter-welcome, in no less degree.

PHEBE [*to* SILVIUS].
  I will not eat my word, now thou art mine;
  Thy faith my fancy to thee doth combine.

     Enter JAQUES DE BOYS.

JAQUES DE BOYS
  Let me have audience for a word or two:
  I am the second son of old Sir Rowland,
  That bring these tidings to this fair assembly. —
  Duke Frederick, hearing how that every day
  Men of great worth resorted to this forest,
  Address'd a mighty power; which were on foot,
  In his own conduct, purposely to take
  His brother here, and put him to the sword:
  And to the skirts of this wild wood he came;
  Where meeting with an old religious man,
  After some question with him, was converted
  Both from his enterprise and from the world;
  His crown bequeathing to his banish'd brother,
  And all their lands restored to them again
  That were with him exil'd. This to be true,
  I do engage my life.

DUKE SENIOR
             Welcome, young man;
  Thou offer'st fairly to thy brothers' wedding:
  To one, his lands withheld; and to the other,
  A land itself at large, a potent dukedom.
  First, in this forest, let us do those ends
  That here were well begun and well begot:
  And after, every of this happy number,
  That have endured shrewd days and nights with us,
  Shall share the good of our returned fortune,
  According to the measure of their states.
  Meantime forget this new-fall'n dignity,

And fall into our rustic revelry. —
Play, music! — and you, brides and bridegrooms all,
With measure heap'd in joy, to th'measures fall.

JAQUES

Sir, by your patience. — If I heard you rightly,
The duke hath put on a religious life,
And thrown into neglect the pompous court?

JAQUES DE BOYS

He hath.

JAQUES

To him will I: out of these convertites
There is much matter to be heard and learn'd. —
You [*to* DUKE SENIOR] to your former honour I
    bequeath;
Your patience and your virtue well deserves it: —
You [*to* ORLANDO] to a love that your true faith doth
    merit: —
You [*to* OLIVER] to your land, and love, and great
    allies: —
You [*to* SILVIUS] to a long and well-deserved bed: —
And you [*to* TOUCHSTONE] to wrangling; for thy
    loving voyage
Is but for two months victuall'd. — So, to your
    pleasures:
I am for other than for dancing measures.

DUKE SENIOR

Stay, Jaques, stay.

JAQUES

To see no pastime I: — what you would have
I'll stay to know at your abandon'd cave.

                                 [*Exit.*

DUKE SENIOR

Proceed, proceed: we will begin these rites,
As we do trust they'll end, in true delights.   [*A dance.*

EPILOGUE

ROSALIND

It is not the fashion to see the lady the epilogue; but it is no more unhandsome than to see the lord the prologue. If it be true that good wine needs no bush, 'tis true that a good play needs no epilogue: yet to good wine they do use good bushes; and good plays prove the better by the help of good epilogues. What a case am I in, then, that am neither a good epilogue, nor cannot insinuate with you in the behalf of a good play! I am not furnish'd like a beggar, therefore to beg will not become me: my way is, to conjure you; and I'll begin with the women. I charge you, O women, for the love you bear to men, to like as much of this play as please you: and I charge you, O men, for the love you bear to women (as I perceive by your simpering, none of you hates them), that between you and the women the play may please. If I were a woman, I would kiss as many of you as had beards that pleased me, complexions that liked me, and breaths that I defied not: and, I am sure, as many as have good beards, or good faces, or sweet breaths, will, for my kind offer, when I make curtsy, bid me farewell. [*Exeunt.*

GLOSSARY

References are given only for words having more than one meaning, the first use of each sense being then noted.

Abate, *v.t.* to diminish. M.N.D. III. 2. 432. Deduct, except. L.L.L. v. 2. 539. Cast down. Cor. III. 3. 134. Blunt. R III. v. 5. 35. Deprive. Lear, II. 4. 159.

Abatement, *sb.* diminution Lear, I. 4. 59. Depreciation. Tw.N. I. 1. 13.

Abjects, *sb.* outcasts, servile persons.

Able, *v.t.* to warrant.

Abode, *v.t.* to forebode. 3 H VI. V. 6. 45.

Abode, *sb.* stay, delay. M. of V. II. 6. 77.

Abodements, *sb.* forebodings.

Abram, *adj.* auburn.

Abridgement, *sb.* short entertainment, for pastime.

Abrook, *v.t.* to brook, endure.

Absey book, *sb.* ABC book, or primer.

Absolute, *adj.* resolved. M. for M. III. 1. 5. Positive. Cor. III. 2. 39. Perfect. H V. III. 7. 26. Complete. Tp. I. 2. 109; Lucr. 853.

Aby, *v.t.* to atone for, expiate.

Accite, *v.t.* to cite, summon.

Acknown, *adj.* cognisant.

Acture, *sb.* performance.

Addition, *sb.* title, attribute.

Adoptious, *adj.* given by adoption.

Advice, *sb.* consideration.

Aery, *sb.* eagle's nest or brood. R III. I. 3. 265, 271. Hence generally any brood. Ham. II. 2. 344.

Affectioned, *p.p.* affected.

Affeered, *p.p.* sanctioned, confirmed.

Affiance, *sb.* confidence, trust.

Affined, *p.p.* related. T. & C. I. 3. 25. Bound. Oth. I. 1. 39.

Affront, *v.t.* to confront, meet.

Affy, v.t. to betroth. 2 H VI. IV . 1. 80. *v.t.* to trust. T.A. I.1. 47.

Aglet-baby, sb. small figure cut on the tag of a lace (Fr. *aiguillette*). T. of S. I. 2. 78.

Agnize, v.t. to acknowledge, confess.

Agood, adv. much.

Aim, sb. a guess.

Aim, to cry aim, to encourage, an archery term.

Alderliefest, adj. most loved of all.

Ale, sb. alehouse.

All amort, completely dejected (Fr. *a la mort*).

Allicholy, sb. melancholy.

Allow, v.t. to approve.

Allowance, sb. acknowledgement, approval.

Ames-ace, sb. the lowest throw of the dice.

Anchor, sb. anchorite, hermit.

Ancient, sb. ensign, standard. 1 H IV. IV. 2. 32. Ensign, ensign-bearer. 1 H IV. IV. 2. 24.

Ancientry, sb. antiquity, used of old people, W.T. III. 3. 62. Of the gravity which belongs to antiquity, M.A. II. 1. 75.

Angel, sb. gold coin, worth about 10s.

Antic, adj. fantastic. Ham. I. 5. 172.

Antick, v.t. to make a buffoon of. A. & C. II. 7. 126.

Antick, sb. buffoon of the old plays.

Appeal, sb. impeachment.

Appeal, v.t. to impeach.

Apperil, sb. peril.

Apple-john, sb. a shrivelled winter apple.

Argal, corruption of the Latin *ergo*, therefore.

Argo, corruption of *ergo*, therefore.

Aroint thee, begone, get thee gone.

Articulate, v.i. to make articles of peace. Cor. I. 9. 75. *v.t.* to set forth in detail. 1 H IV. V. 1. 72.

Artificial, adj. working by art.

Askance, v.t. to make look askance or sideways, make to avert.

Aspic, sb. asp.

Assured, p.p. betrothed.

Atone, v.t. to reconcile. R II. I. 1. 202. Agree. As V. 4. 112.

Attorney, *sb.* proxy, agent.

Attorneyed, *p.p.* done by proxy. W T. I. 1. 28. Engaged as
   an attorney, M. for M. V. 1. 383.

Attribute, *sb.* reputation.

Avail, *sb.* profit.

Avise, *v.t.* to inform. Are you avised? = Do you know?

Awful, *adj.* filled with regard for authority.

Awkward, *adj.* contrary.

Baby, *sb.* a doll.

Baccare, go back, a spurious Latin word.

Back-trick, a caper backwards in dancing.

Baffle, *v.t.* to disgrace (a recreant knight).

Bale, *sb.* evil, mischief.

Ballow, *sb.* cudgel.

Ban, *v.t.* curse. 2 H VI. II. 4. 25. *sb.* a curse. Ham. III. 2. 269.

Band, *sb.* bond.

Bank, *v.t.* sail along the banks of.

Bare, *v.t.* to shave.

Barn, *v.t.* to put in a barn.

Barn, or Barne, *sb.* bairn, child.

Base, *sb.* a rustic game. Bid the base = Challenge to a race.
   Two G. I. 2. 97.

Bases, *sb.* knee-length skirts worn by mounted knights.

Basilisco-like, Basilisco, a character in the play of *Soliman
   and Perseda.*

Basilisk, *sb.* a fabulous serpent. H V. V. 2. 17. A large
   cannon. 1 H IV. II. 3. 57.

Bate, *sb.* strife.

Bate, *v.i.* flutter as a hawk. 1 H IV. IV. 1. 99. Diminish. 1 H
   IV. III. 3. 2.

Bate, *v.t.* abate. Tp. I. 2. 250. Beat down, weaken. M. of V.
   III. 3. 32.

Bavin, *adj.* made of bavin or brushwood. 1 H IV. III. 2. 61.

Bawbling, *adj.* trifling, insignificant.

Baw-cock, *sb.* fine fellow (Fr. *beau coq.*) H V. III. 2. 25.

Bay, *sb.* space between the main timbers in a roof.

Beadsman, *sb.* one who is hired to offer prayers for another.

Bearing-cloth, *sb.* the cloth in which a child was carried to be christened.

Bear in hand, to deceive with false hopes.

Beat, *v.i.* to meditate. 2 H IV. II. 1. 20. Throb. Lear, III. 4. 14.

Becoming, *sb.* grace.

Beetle, *sb.* a heavy mallet, 2 H IV. I. 2. 235. Beetle-headed = heavy, stupid. T. of S. IV. 1. 150.

Behave, *v.t.* to control.

Behest, *sb.* command.

Behove, *sb.* behoof.

Be-lee'd, *p.p.* forced to lee of the wind.

Bench, *v.i.* to seat on the bench of justice. Lear, III. 6. 38. *v.t.* to elevate to the bench. W.T. I .2. 313.

Bench-hole, the hole of a privy.

Bergomask, a rustic dance, named from Bergamo in Italy.

Beshrew, *v.t.* to curse; but not used seriously.

Besort, *v.t.* to fit, suit.

Bestraught, *adj.* distraught.

Beteem, *v.t.* to permit, grant.

Bezonian, *sb.* a base and needy fellow.

Bias, *adj.* curving like the bias side of a bowling bowl.

Biggen, *sb.* a nightcap.

Bilbo, *sb.* a Spanish rapier, named from Bilbao or Bilboa.

Bilboes, *sb.* stocks used for punishment on shipboard.

Birdbolt, *sb.* a blunt-headed arrow used for birds.

Bisson, *adj.* dim-sighted. Cor. II. 1. 65. Bisson rheum = blinding tears. Ham. II. 2. 514.

Blacks, *sb.* black mourning clothes.

Blank, *sb.* the white mark in the centre of a target.

Blank, *v.t.* to blanch, make pale.

Blanks, *sb.* royal charters left blank to be filled in as occasion dictated.

Blench, *sb.* a swerve, inconsistency.

Blistered, *adj.* padded out, puffed.

Block, *sb.* the wood on which hats are made. M.A. I. 1. 71. Hence, the style of hat. Lear, IV. 6. 185.

Blood-boltered, *adj*. clotted with blood.

Blowse, *sb*. a coarse beauty.

Bob, *sb*. smart rap, jest.

Bob, *v.t*. to beat hard, thwack. R III. V. 3. 335. To obtain by fraud, cheat. T. & C. III. 1. 69.

Bodge, *v.i*. to budge.

Bodkin, *sb*. small dagger, stiletto.

Boggle, *v.i*. to swerve, shy, hesitate.

Boggler, *sb*. swerver.

Boln, *adj*. swollen.

Bolt, *v.t*. to sift, refine.

Bolter, *sb*. a sieve.

Bombard, *sb*. a leathern vessel for liquor.

Bona-robas, *sb*. flashily dressed women of easy virtue.

Bonnet, *v.i*. to doff the hat, be courteous.

Boot, *sb*. profit. 1 H VI. IV. 6. 52. That which is given over and above. R III. IV. 4. 65. Booty. 3 H VI. IV. 1. 13.

Boots, *sb*. Give me not the boots = do not inflict on me the torture of the boots, which were employed to wring confessions.

Bosky, *adj*. woody.

Botcher, *sb*. patcher of old clothes.

Bots, *sb*. small worms in horses.

Bottled, *adj*. big-bellied.

Brabble, *sb*. quarrel, brawl.

Brabbler, *sb*. a brawler.

Brach, *sb*. a hound-bitch.

Braid, *adj*. deceitful.

Braid, *v.t*. to upbraid, reproach.

Brain, *v.t*. to conceive in the brain.

Brazed, *p.p*. made like brass, perhaps hardened in the fire.

Breeched, *p.p*. as though wearing breeches. Mac. II. 3. 120.

Breeching, *adj*. liable to be breeched for a flogging.

Breese, *sb*. a gadfly.

Brib'd-buck, *sb*. perhaps a buck distributed in presents.

Brock, *sb*. badger.

Broken, *adj*. of a mouth with some teeth missing.

Broker, *sb.* agent, go-between.

Brownist, a follower of Robert Brown, the founder of the sect of Independents.

Buck, *v.t.* to wash and beat linen.

Buck-basket, *sb.* a basket to take linen to be bucked.

Bucking, *sb.* washing.

Buckle, *v.i.* to encounter hand to hand, cope. 1. H VI. I. 2. 95. To bow. 2 H VI. I. 1. 141.

Budget, *sb.* a leather scrip or bag.

Bug, *sb.* bugbear, a thing causing terror.

Bugle, *sb.* a black bead.

Bully, *sb.* a fine fellow.

Bully-rook, *sb.* a swaggering cheater.

Bung, *sb.* pickpocket.

Burgonet, *sb.* close-fitting Burgundian helmet.

Busky, *adj.* woody.

By-drinkings, *sb.* drinks taken between meals.

Caddis, *sb.* worsted trimming, galloon.

Cade, *sb.* cask, barrel.

Caitiff, *sb.* captive, slave, a wretch. *adj.* R II. I. 2. 53.

Caliver, *sb.* musket.

Callet, *sb.* trull, drab.

Calling, *sb.* appellation.

Calm, *sb.* qualm.

Canaries = quandary.

Canary, *sb.* a lively Spanish dance. *v.i.* to dance canary.

Canker, *sb.* the dog-rose or wild-rose. 1 H IV. I. 3. 176. A worm that destroys blossoms. M.N.D. II. 2.3.

Canstick, *sb.* candlestick.

Cantle, *sb.* piece, slice.

Canton, *sb.* canto.

Canvass, *v.t.* shake as in a sieve, take to task.

Capable, *adj.* sensible. As III. 5. 23. Sensitive, susceptible. Ham. III. 4. 128. Comprehensive. Oth. III. 3. 459. Able to possess. Lear, II. 1. 85.

Capocchia, *sb.* the feminine of capocchio (Ital.), simpleton.

Capriccio, *sb.* caprice, fancy.

Captious, *adj.* either a contraction of capacious or a coined word meaning capable of receiving.

Carack, *sb.* a large merchant ship.

Carbonado, *sb.* meat scotched for boiling. *v.t.* to hack like a carbonado.

Card, *sb.* a cooling card = a sudden and decisive stroke.

Card, *v.t.* to mix (liquids).

Cardecu, *sb.* quarter of a French crown (*quart d'écu*).

Care, *v.i.* to take care.

Careire, career, *sb.* a short gallop at full speed.

Carlot, *sb.* peasant.

Carpet consideration, On, used of those made knights for court services, not for valour in the field.

Carpet-mongers, *sb.* carpet-knights.

Carpets, *sb.* tablecloths.

Case, *v.t.* to strip off the case or skin of an animal. A.W. III. 6. 103. Put on a mask. 1 H IV. II. 2. 55.

Case, *sb.* skin of an animal. Tw.N. V. 1.163. A set, as of musical instruments, which were in fours. H V. III. 2. 4.

Cashiered, *p.p.* discarded; in M.W.W. I. 1. 168 it probably means relieved of his cash.

Cataian, *sb.* a native of Cathay, a Chinaman; a cant word.

Cater-cousins, good friends.

Catlings, *sb.* catgut strings for musical instruments.

Cautel, *sb.* craft, deceit, stratagem.

Cautelous, *adj.* crafty, deceitful.

Ceased, *p.p.* put off.

Censure, *sb.* opinion, judgement.

Certify, *v.t.* to inform, make certain.

Cess, *sb.* reckoning; out of all cess = immoderately.

Cesse = cease.

Champain, *sb.* open country.

Channel, *sb.* gutter.

Chape, *sb.* metal end of a scabbard.

Chapless, *adj.* without jaws.

Charact, *sb.* a special mark or sign of office.

Chare, *sb.* a turn of work.

Charge, *sb.* weight, importance. W.T. IV. 3. 258. Cost, expense. John I. 1. 49.

Chaudron, *sb.* entrails.

Check, *sb.* rebuke, reproof.

Check, *v.t.* to rebuke, chide.

Check, *v.i.* to start on sighting game.

Cherry-pit, *sb.* a childish game consisting of pitching cherry-stones into a small hole.

Cheveril, *sb.* leather of kid skin. R. & J. II. 3. 85. *adj.* Tw.N. III. 1. 12.

Che vor ye = I warn you.

Chewet, *sb.* chough. 1 H IV. V. 1. 29. (Fr. *chouette* or *chutte*). Perhaps with play on other meaning of chewet, *i.e.*, a kind of meat pie.

Childing, *adj.* fruitful.

Chop, *v.t.* to clop, pop.

Chopine, *sb.* shoe with a high sole.

Choppy, *adj.* chapped.

Christendom, *sb.* Christian name.

Chuck, *sb.* chick, term of endearment.

Chuff, *sb.* churl, boor.

Cinque pace, *sb.* a slow stately dance. M.A. II. 1. 72. Compare sink-a-pace in Tw.N. I. 3. 126.

Cipher, *v.t.* to decipher.

Circumstance, *sb.* particulars, details. Two G. I. 1. 36. Ceremonious phrases. M. of V. I. 1. 154.

Circumstanced, *p.p.* swayed by circumstance.

Citizen, *adj.* town-bred, effeminate.

Cittern, *sb.* guitar.

Clack-dish, *sb.* wooden dish carried by beggars.

Clamour, *v.t.* to silence.

Clapper-claw, *v.t.* to thrash, drub.

Claw, *v.t.* to scratch, flatter.

Clepe, *v.t.* to call.

Cliff, *sb.* clef, the key in music.

Cling, *v.t.* to make shrivel up.

Clinquant, *adj.* glittering with gold or silver lace or decorations.

Close, *sb.* cadence in music. R II. II. 1. 12. *adj.* secret. T. of S. Ind. I. 127. *v.i.* to come to an agreement, make terms. Two G. II. 5. 12.

Closely, *adv.* secretly.

Clout, *sb.* bull's-eye of a target.

Clouted, *adj.* hobnailed (others explain as patched).

Cobloaf, *sb.* a crusty, ill-shapen loaf.

Cockered, *p.p.* pampered.

Cockle, *sb.* the corncockle weed.

Cockney, *sb.* a city-bred person, a foolish wanton.

Cock-shut time, *sb.* twilight.

Codding, *adj.* lascivious.

Codling, *sb.* an unripe apple.

Cog, *v.i.* to cheat. R III I. 3. 48. *v.t.* to get by cheating, filch. Cor. III. 2. 133.

Coistrel, *sb.* groom.

Collection, *sb.* inference.

Collied, *p.p.* blackened, darkened.

Colour, *sb.* pretext. Show no colour, or bear no colour = allow of no excuse.

Colours, fear no colours = fear no enemy, be afraid of nothing.

Colt, *v.t.* to make a fool of, gull.

Combinate, *adj.* betrothed.

Combine, *v.t.* to bind.

Comfect, *sb.* comfit.

Commodity, *sb.* interest, advantage. John, II. 1. 573. Cargo of merchandise. Tw.N. III. 1. 46.

Comparative, *adj.* fertile in comparisons. 1 H IV. I. 2. 83.

Comparative, *sb.* a rival in wit. 1 H IV. III. 2. 67.

Compassed, *adj.* arched, round.

Complexion, *sb.* temperament.

Comply, *v.i.* to be ceremonious.

Composition, *sb.* agreement, consistency.

Composture, *sb.* compost.

Composure, *sb.* composition. T. & C. II. 3. 238; A. & C. I. 4. 22. Compact. T. & C. II. 3. 100.

Compt. *sb.* account, reckoning.

Comptible, *adj.* susceptible, sensitive.

Con, *v.t.* to study, learn; con thanks = give thanks.

Conceptious, *adj.* apt at conceiving.

Conclusion, *sb.* experiment.

Condolement, *sb.* lamentation. Ham. I. 2. 93. Consolation, Per. II. 1. 150.

Conduce, *v.i.* perhaps to tend to happen.

Conduct, *sb.* guide, escort.

Confiners, *sb.* border peoples.

Confound, *v.t.* to waste. 1 H IV. I. 3. 100. Destroy. M. of V. III. 2. 278.

Congied, *p.p.* taken leave (Fr. *congé*).

Consent, *sb.* agreement, plot.

Consist, *v.i.* to insist.

Consort, *sb.* company, fellowship. Two G. III. 2. 84; IV. 1. 64. *v.t.* to accompany. C. of E. I. 2. 28.

Conspectuity, *sb.* power of vision.

Constant, *adj.* consistent.

Constantly, *adv.* firmly, surely.

Conster, *v.t.* to construe, interpret.

Constringed, *p.p.* compressed.

Consul, *sb.* senator.

Containing, *sb.* contents.

Contraction, *sb.* the making of the marriage-contract.

Contrive, *v.t.* to wear out, spend. T. of S. I. 2. 273. Conspire. J.C. II. 3. 16.

Control, *v.t.* to check, contradict.

Convent, *v.t.* to summon.

Convert, *v.i.* to change.

Convertite, *sb.* a penitent.

Convince, *v.t.* to overcome. Mac. I. 7. 64. Convict. T. & C. II. 2. 130.

Convive, *v.i.* to banquet together.

Convoy, *sb.* conveyance, escort.

Copatain hat, *sb.* a high-crowned hat.

Cope, *v.t.* to requite. M. of V. IV. 1. 412.

Copesmate, *sb.* a companion.

Copped, *adj.* round-topped.

Copulatives, *sb.* persons desiring to be coupled in marriage.

Copy, *sb.* theme, text. C. of E. V. 1. 62. Tenure. Mac. III. 2. 37.

Coranto, *sb.* a quick, lively dance.

Corky, *adj.* shrivelled (with age).

Cornet, *sb.* a band of cavalry.

Corollary, *sb.* a supernumerary.

Cosier, *sb.* botcher, cobbler.

Costard, *sb.* an apple, the head (slang).

Cote, *v.t.* to come up with, pass on the way.

Cot-quean, *sb.* a man who busies himself in women's affairs.

Couch, *v.t.* to make to cower.

Counter, *adv.* to run or hunt counter is to trace the scent of the game backwards.

Counter, *sb.* a metal disk used in reckoning.

Counter-caster, *sb.* one who reckons by casting up counters.

Countermand, *v.t.* to prohibit, keep in check. C. of E. IV. 2. 37. Contradict. Lucr. 276.

Countervail, *v.t.* to outweigh.

County, *sb.* count. As II. 1. 67.

Couplet, *sb.* a pair.

Courser's hair, a horse's hair laid in water was believed to turn into a serpent.

Court holy-water, *sb.* flattery.

Courtship, *sb.* courtly manners.

Convent, *sb.* a convent.

Cox my passion = God's passion.

Coy, *v.t.* to fondle, caress. M.N.D. IV. 1. 2. *v.i.* to disdain. Cor. V. 1. 6.

Crack, *v.i.* to boast. *sb.* an urchin.

Crank, *sb.* winding passage. *v.i.* to wind, twist.

Crants, *sb.* garland, chaplet.

Crare, *sb.* a small sailing vessel.

Crisp, *adj.* curled.

Cross, *sb.* a coin (stamped with a cross).

Cross-row, *sb.* alphabet.

Crow-keeper, *sb.* a boy, or scare-crow, to keep crows from corn.

Cullion, *sb.* a base fellow.

Cunning, *sb.* knowledge, skill. *adj.* knowing, skilful, skilfully wrought.

Curb, *v.i.* to bow, cringe obsequiously.

Curdied, *p.p.* congealed.

Curiosity, *sb.* scrupulous nicety.

Curst, *adj.* bad-tempered.

Curtal, *adj.* having a docked tail. *sb.* a dock-tailed horse.

Customer, *sb.* a loose woman.

Cut, *sb.* a bobtailed horse.

Cuttle, *sb.* a bully.

Daff, *v.t.* to doff. Daff aside = thrust aside slightingly.

Darraign, *v.t.* to arrange, order the ranks for battle.

Dash, *sb.* mark of disgrace.

Daubery, *sb.* false pretence, cheat.

Day-woman, *sb.* dairy-woman.

Debosht, *p.p.* debauched.

Deck, *sb.* pack of cards.

Deem, *sb.* doom; opinion.

Defeat, *v.t.* to disguise. Oth. I. 3. 333. Destroy. Oth. IV. 2. 160.

Defeature, *sb.* disfigurement.

Defend, *v.t.* to forbid.

Defuse, *v.t.* to disorder and make unrecognizable.

Defused, *p.p.* disordered, shapeless.

Demerit, *sb.* desert.

Denier, *sb.* a small French coin.

Dern, *adj.* secret, dismal.

Detect, *v.t.* to discover, disclose.

Determinate, *p.p.* determined upon. Tw.N. II. 1. 10. Decided. Oth. IV. 2. 229. Ended. Sonn. LXXXVII. 4. *v.t.* bring to an end. R II. 1. 3.

Dich, *v.i.* do to, happen to.

Diet, *v.t.* keep strictly, as if by a prescribed regimen.

Diffidence, *sb.* distrust, suspicion.

Digression, *sb.* transgression.

Diminutives, *sb.* the smallest of coins.

Directitude, *sb.* a blunder for some word unknown. Cor. IV. 5. 205.

Disanimate, *v.t.* to discourage.

Disappointed, *p.p.* unprepared.

Discandy, *v.i.* to thaw, melt.

Discipled, *p.p.* taught.

Disclose, *v.t.* to hatch. *sb.* the breaking of the shell by the chick on hatching.

Disme, *sb.* a tenth.

Distain, *v.t.* to stain, pollute.

Dive-dapper, *sb.* dabchick.

Dividant, *adj.* separate, different.

Dotant, *sb.* dotard.

Doubt, *sb.* fear, apprehension.

Dout, *v.t.* to extinguish.

Dowlas, *sb.* coarse linen.

Dowle, *sb.* down, the soft plumage of a feather.

Down-gyved, *adj.* hanging down about the ankle like gyves.

Dribbling, *adj.* weakly shot.

Drugs, *sb.* drudges.

Drumble, *v.i.* to be sluggish or clumsy.

Dry-beat, *v.t.* to cudgel, thrash.

Dry-foot. To draw dry-foot, track by scent.

Dudgeon, *sb.* the handle of a dagger.

Due, *v.t.* to endue.

Dump, *sb.* a sad strain.

Dup, *v.t.* to open.

Ean, *v.i.* to yean, lamb.

Ear, *v.t.* to plough, till.

Eche, *v.t.* to eke out.

Eftest, *adv.* readiest.

Eftsoons, *adv.* immediately.

Egal, *adj.* equal.

Egally, *adv.* equally.

Eisel, *sb.* vinegar.

Elf, *v.t.* to mat hair in a tangle; believed to be the work of elves.

Emballing, *sb.* investiture with the crown and sceptre.

Embarquement, *sb.* hindrance, restraint.

Ember-eyes, *sb.* vigils of Ember days.

Embowelled, *p.p.* emptied, exhausted.

Emmew, *v.t.* perhaps to mew up.

Empiricutic, *adj.* empirical, quackish.

Emulation, *sb.* jealous rivalry.

Enacture, *sb.* enactment, performance.

Encave, *v.t.* to hide, conceal.

Encumbered, *p.p.* folded.

End, *sb.* still an end = continually.

End, *v.t.* to get in the harvest.

Englut, *v.t.* to swallow.

Enlargement, *sb.* liberty, liberation.

Enormous, *adj.* out of the norm, monstrous.

Enseamed, *p.p.* defiled, filthy.

Ensear, *v.t.* to sear up, make dry.

Enshield, *adj.* enshielded, protected.

Entertain, *v.t.* to take into one's service.

Entertainment, *sb.* service.

Entreat, *v.t.* to treat.

Entreatments, *sb.* invitations.

Ephesian, *sb.* boon companion.

Eryngoes, *sb.* roots of the sea-holly, a supposed aphrodisiac.

Escot, *v.t.* to pay for.

Espial, *sb.* a spy.

Even Christian, *sb.* fellow Christian.

Excrement, *sb.* anything that grows out of the body, as hair, nails, etc. Used of the beard. M. of V. III. 2. 84. Of the hair. C. of E. II. 2. 79. Of the moustache. L.L.L. V. 1. 98.

Exhibition, *sb.* allowance, pension.

Exigent, *sb.* end. 1 H VI. II. 5. 9. Exigency, critical need. J. C. V. I. 19.

Exion, *sb.* blunder for action.

Expiate, *v.t* . to terminate. Sonn. XXII. 4.

Expiate, *p.p.* ended. R III. III. 3. 24.

Exsufflicate, *adj.* inflated, both literally and metaphorically.

Extent, *sb.* seizure. As III. 1. 17. Violent attack. Tw.N. IV. 1. 51. Condescension, favour. Ham. II. 2. 377. Display. T. A. IV. 4. 3.

Extraught, *p.p.* extracted.

Extravagancy, *sb.* vagrancy, aimless wandering about.

Eyas, *sb.* a nestling, a young hawk just taken from the nest.

Eyas-musket, *sb.* the young sparrow-hawk.

Eye, *v.i.* to appear, look to the eye.

Facinerious, *adj.* wicked.

Fadge, *v.i.* to succeed, suit.

Fading, *sb.* the burden of a song.

Fair, *v.t.* to make beautiful.

Fairing, *sb.* a gift.

Faitor, *sb.* evil-doer.

Fangled, *adj.* fond of novelties.

Fap, *adj.* drunk.

Farced, *p.p.* stuffed out.

Fardel, *sb.* a burden, bundle.

Fat, *adj.* cloying. *sb.* vat.

Favour, *sb.* outward appearance, aspect. In pl. = features.

Fear, *v.t.* to frighten. 3 H VI. III. 3. 226. Fear for. M. of V. III. 5. 3.

Feat, *adj.* neat, dexterous.

Feat, *v.t.* to fashion, form.

Fee, *sb.* worth, value.

Feeder, *sb.* servant.

Fee-farm, *sb.* a tenure without limit of time.

Fellowly, *adj.* companionable, sympathetic.

Feodary, *sb.* confederate.

Fere, *sb.* spouse, consort.

Ferret, *v.t.* to worry.

Festinate, *adj.* swift, speedy.

Fet, *p.p.* fetched.

Fico, *sb.* a fig (Span.).

File, *sb.* list.

File, *v.t.* to defile. Mac. III. 1. 65. Smooth, polish. L.L.L. V.
   1. 11. *v.i.*to walk in file. H VIII. III. 2. 171.

Fill-horse, *sb.* a shaft-horse.

Fills, *sb.* shafts.

Fineless, *adj.* endless, infinite.

Firago, *sb.* virago.

Firk, *v.t.* to beat.

Fitchew, *sb.* pole-cat.

Fitment, *sb.* that which befits.

Flap-dragon, *sb.* snap-dragon, or small burning object,
   lighted and floated in a glass of liquor, to be swallowed
   burning. L.L.L. V. 1. 43. 2 H IV. II. 4. 244. *v.t.* to swallow
   like a flap-dragon. W.T. III. 3.100.

Flaw, *sb.* gust of wind. Ham. V. 1. 223. Small flake of ice. 2
   H IV. IV. 4. 35. Passionate outburst. M. for M. II. 3. 11. A
   crack. Lear, II. 4. 288. *v.t.* make a flaw in, break. H VIII.
   I. 1. 95; I. 2. 21.

Fleer, *sb.* sneer. Oth. IV. 1. 83. *v.i.* to grin; sneer. L.L.L. V.
   2. 109.

Fleshment, *sb.* encouragement given by first success.

Flewed, *p.p.* with large hanging chaps.

Flight, *sb.* a long light arrow.

Flighty, *adj.* swift.

Flirt-gill, *sb.* light wench.

Flote, *sb.* sea.

Flourish, *v.t.* to ornament, gloss over.

Fobbed, *p.p.* cheated, deceived.

Foil, *sb.* defeat. 1 H VI. III. 3. 11. *v.t.* to defeat, mar. Pass.
   P. 99

Foin, *v.i.* to thrust (in fencing).

Fopped, *p.p.* cheated, fooled.

Forbod, *p.p.* forbidden.

Fordo, *v.t.* to undo, destroy.

Foreign, *adj.* dwelling abroad.

Fork, *sb.* the forked tongue of a snake. M. for M. III. 1. 16. The barbed head of an arrow. Lear, I. 1. 146. The junction of the legs with the trunk. Lear. IV. 6. 120.

Forked, *p.p.* barbed. As II. 1. 24. Horned as a cuckold. T. & C. I. 2. 164.

Forslow, *v.i.* to delay.

Forspeak, *v.t.* to speak against.

Fosset-seller, *sb.* a seller of taps.

Fox, *sb.* broadsword.

Foxship, *sb.* selfish and ungrateful, cunning.

Fracted, *p.p.* broken.

Frampold, *adj.* turbulent, quarrelsome.

Frank, *v.t.* to pen in a frank or sty. R III. I. 3. 314. *sb.* a sty. 2 H IV. II. 2. 145. *adj.* liberal. Lear, III. 4. 20.

Franklin, *sb.* a yeoman.

Fraught, *sb.* freight, cargo, load. Tw.N. V. 1. 59. *v.t.* to load, burden. Cym. I. 1. 126. *p.p.* laden. M. of V. II. 8. 30. Stored. Two G. III. 2. 70.

Fraughtage, *sb.* cargo. C. of E. IV. 1. 8.

Fraughting, *part. adj.* constituting the cargo.

Frize, *sb.* a kind of coarse woollen cloth with a nap.

Frontier, *sb.* an outwork in fortification. 1 H IV. II. 3. 56. Used figuratively. 1 H IV. I. 3. 19.

Fruitful, *adj.* bountiful, plentiful.

Frush, *v.t.* to bruise, batter.

Frutify, blunder for certify. M. of V II. 2. 132.

Fubbed off, *p.p.* put off with excuses. 2 H IV. II. 1. 34.

Fullams, *sb.* a kind of false dice.

Gad, *sb.* a pointed instrument. T.A. IV. 1. 104. Upon the gad = on the spur of the moment, hastily. Lear, I. 2. 26.

Gage, *v.t.* to pledge.

Gaingiving, *sb.* misgiving.

Galliard, *sb.* a lively dance.

Gallimaufry, *sb.* medley, tumble.

Gallow, *v.t.* to frighten.

Gallowglass, *sb.* heavy- armed Irish foot-soldier.

Gallows, *sb.* a rogue, one fit to be hung.

Gallows-bird, *sb.* one that merits hanging.

Garboil, *sb.* uproar, commotion.

Gaskins, *sb.* loose breeches.

Gastness, *sb.* ghastliness, terror.

Geck, *sb.* dupe.

Generation, *sb.* offspring.

Generous, *adj.* nobly born.

Gennet, *sb.* a Spanish horse.

Gentry, *sb.* rank by birth. M.W. W. II. 1. 51. Courtesy. Ham. II. 2. 22.

German, *sb.* a near kinsman.

Germen, *sb.* germ, seed.

Gest, *sb.* a period of sojourn; originally the halting place in a royal progress.

Gib, *sb.* an old rom-cat.

Gibbet, *v.t.* to hang, as a barrel when it is slung.

Gig, *sb.* top.

Giglot, *adj.* wanton. 1 H VI. IV. 7. 41. *sb.* M. for M. V. 1. 345.

Gillyvors, *sb.* gillyflowers.

Gimmal-bit, *sb.* a double bit, or one made with double rings.

Gimmer, *sb.* contrivance, mechanical device.

Ging, *sb.* gang, pack.

Gird, *sb.* a scoff, jest. 2 H VI. III. 1. 131. *v.t.* to taunt, gibe at. 2 H IV. I. 2. 6.

Gleek, *sb.* scoff. 1 H VI. IV. 2. 12. *v.i.* to scoff. M.N.D. III. 1. 145.

Glib, *v.t.* to geld.

Gloze, *v.i.* to comment. H V. I. 2. 40. T. & C. II. 2. 165. To use flattery. R II. II. 1. 10; T.A. IV. 4. 35.

Gnarling, *pr.p.* snarling.

Godden, *sb.* good den, good even.

God'ild, God yield, God reward.

God-jer = good-year.

Good-year, *sb.* a meaningless interjection. M.A. I. 3. I. Some malific power. Lear, V. 3. 24.

Goss, *sb.* gorse.

Gossip, *sb.* sponsor. Two G. III. 1. 269. *v.t.* to stand sponsor for. A. W. I. 1. 176.

Gorbellied, *adj.* big-bellied.

Graff, *sb.* graft, scion. *v.t.* to graft.

Grain, *sb.* a fast colour. Hence in grain = ingrained.

Gratillity, *sb.* gratuity.

Gratulate, *adj.* gratifying.

Greek, *sb.* boon companion.

Grise, *sb.* a step.

Guard, *v.t.* to trim, ornament.

Guardant, *sb.* sentinel, guard.

Guidon, *sb.* standard, banner.

Gules, *adj.* red, in heraldry.

Gust, *sb.* taste. *v.t.* to taste.

Hackney, *sb.* loose woman.

Haggard, *sb.* untrained hawk.

Haggled, *p.p.* hacked, mangled.

Hair, *sb.* texture, nature. 1 H IV. IV. 1. 61. Against the hair = against the grain. R. & J. II. 3. 97.

Handfast, *sb.* betrothal, contract. Cym. I. 5. 78. Custody. W.T. IV. 3. 778.

Handsaw, *sb.* corruption of heronshaw, a heron.

Hardiment, *sb.* daring deed.

Harlot, *adj.* lewd, base.

Hatched, *p.p.* closed with a hatch or half door. Per. IV. 2. 33. Engraved. T. & C. I. 3. 65.

Havoc, to cry havoc = cry no quarter. John, II. 1. 357. *v.t.* cut to pieces, destroy. H V. I. 2. 193.

Hawking, *adj.* hawk-like.

Hay, *sb.* a round dance. L.L.L. V. 1. 147. A term in fencing when a hit is made (Ital. *hai*, you have it). R. & J. II. 4. 27.

Hebenon, *sb.* perhaps the yew (Germ. *Eiben*). Ebony and henbane have been suggested.

Hefts, *sb.* heavings.

Helm, *v.t.* to steer.

Helpless, *adj.* not helping, useless. R III. I. 2. 13; Lucr. 1027. Incurable, Lucr. 756.

Hent, *sb.* grasp, hold. Ham. III. 3. 88. *v.t.* to hold, pass. M. for M. IV. 6. 14.

Hermit, *sb.* beadsman, one bound to pray for another.

Hild = held.

Hilding, *sb.* a good-for-nothing.

Hoar, *adj.* mouldy, R. & J. II. 3. 136. *v.i.* to become mouldy. R. & J. II. 3. 142.

Hoar, *v.t.* to make hoary or white, as with leprosy.

Hobby-horse, *sb.* a principal figure in the old morris dance. L.L.L. III. 1. 30. A light woman. M.A. III. 2. 68.

Hob-nob, have or not have, hit or miss.

Hold in, *v.i.* to keep counsel.

Holding, *sb.* the burden of a song. A. & C. II. 7. 112. Fitness, sense. A.W. IV. 2. 27.

Holy-ales, *sb.* rural festivals.

Honest, *adj.* chaste.

Honesty, *sb.* chastity. M.W.W. II. 2. 234. Decency. Tw.N. II. 3. 85. Generosity, liberality. Tim. III. 1. 30.

Honey-seed, blunder for homicide, 2 H IV. II. 1. 52.

Honey-suckle, blunder for homicidal. 2 H IV. II. 1. 50.

Hoodman, *sb.* the person blinded in the game of hoodman-blind.

Hoodman-blind, *sb.* blind-man's buff.

Hot at hand, not to be held in.

Hot-house, *sb.* bagnio, often in fact a brothel as well.

Hox, *v.t.* to hough, hamstring.

Hoy, *sb.* a small coasting vessel.

Hugger-mugger, In, stealthily and secretly.

Hull, *v.i.* to float.

Hulling, *pr. p.* floating at the mercy of the waves.

Ignomy, *sb.* ignominy.

Imbar, *v.t.* to bar in, make secure. H V. I. 2. 94.

Imboss, *v.t.* to hunt to death.

Imbossed, *p.p.* swollen. As II. 7. 67. Foaming at the mouth. T. of S. Ind. I. 16.

Immanity, *sb.* savageness, ferocity.

Immoment, *adj.* insignificant.

Immures, *sb.* surrounding walls.

Imp, *v.t.* to graft new feathers to a falcon's wing.

Impair, *adj.* unsuitable.

Impale, *v.t.* to encircle.

Impart, *v.t.* to afford, grant. Lucr. 1039; Sonn. LXXII. 8. *v.i.* to behave oneself. Ham. I. 2. 112.

Imperceiverant, *adj.* lacking in perception.

Impeticos, *v.t.* to put in the petticoat or pocket.

Importance, *sb.* importunity. John, II. 1. 7. Import. W.T. V. 2. 19. Question at issue, that which is imported. Cym. I. 5. 40.

Imposition, *sb.* command, injunction. M. of V. I. 2. 106. Penalty. M. for M. I. 2. 186.

Imposthume, *sb.* abscess.

Imprese, *sb.* device with a motto.

Include, *v.t.* to conclude, end.

Incontinent, *adj.* immediate.

Incony, *adj.* dainty, delicate.

Indent, *v.i.* to make terms.

Index, *sb.* introduction (in old books the index came first).

Indifferency, *sb.* impartiality.

Indirectly, *adv.* wrongly, unjustly.

Indurance, *sb.* durance, imprisonment.

Infest, *v.t.* to vex, trouble.

Inherit, *v.t.* to possess. Tp. IV. 1. 154. To cause to possess, put in possession. R II. I. 1. 85. *v.i.* to take possession. Tp. II. 2. 182.

Inheritor, *sb.* possessor.

Injury, *sb.* insult.

Inkhorn mate, *sb.* bookworm.

Inkle, *sb.* coarse tape.

Insisture, *sb.* persistence.

Intenible, *adj.* incapable of holding.

Intention, *sb.* aim, direction.

Intermissive, *adj.* intermitted, interrupted.

Intrinse, *adj.* tightly drawn.

Invised, *adj.* unseen, a doubtful word.

Irregulous, *adj.* lawless.

Jack, *sb.* figure that struck the bell in old clocks. R III. IV. 2. 114. A term of contempt. R III. I. 3. 72. The small bowl aimed at in the game of bowls. Cym. II. 1. 2. The key of a virginal. Sonn. CXXVIII. 5. A drinking vessel. T. of S. IV. 1. 48.

Jade, *v.t.* to play the jade with, run away with. Tw.N. II. 5. 164. Drive like a jade. A. & C. III. 1. 34. Treat with contempt. H VIII. III. 2. 280.

Jakes, *sb.* a privy.

Jar, *sb.* a tick of the clock. W.T. I. 2. 43.

Jar, *v.t.* to tick. R II. V. 5. 51. *v.i.* to guard. 1 H VI. III. 1. 70. *sb.* a quarrel. 1 H VI. I. 1. 44.

Jesses, *sb.* straps attaching the legs of a hawk to the fist.

Jet, *v.i.* to strut. Tw.N. II. 4. 32. Advance threateningly. R III. II. 4. 51.

Journal, *adj.* diurnal, daily.

Jowl, *v.t.* to knock, dash.

Kam, *adj.* crooked, away from the point.

Keech, *sb.* a lump of tallow or fat.

Keel, *v.t.* to cool.

Ken, *sb.* perception, sight. *v.t.* to know.

Kern, *sb.* light-armed foot-soldier of Ireland.

Kibe, *sb.* chilblain on the heel.

Kicky-wicky, *sb.* a pet name.

Killen = to kill.

Kiln-hole, *sb.* the fireplace of an oven or kiln.

Kind, *sb.* nature. M. of V. I. 3. 84. *adj.* natural. Lucr. 1423.
  adv. kindly. Tim. I. 2. 224.

Kindle, *v.t.* to bring forth young. As III. 2. 343. Incite. As I.
  1. 179.

Knack, *sb.* a pretty trifle.

Knap, *v.t.* to gnaw, nibble. M. of V. III. 1. 9. Rap. Lear, II.
  4. 123.

Laboursome, *adj.* elaborate.

Laced mutton, *sb.* slang for courtesan.

Lade, *v.t.* to empty, drain.

Land-damn. Unrecognizably corrupt word in W.T. II. 1.
  143.

Lapsed, *p.p.* caught, surprised. Tw.N. III. 3. 36.

Latch, *v.t.* to catch, lay hold of.

Latten, *sb.* a mixture of copper and tin. M.W.W. I. 1. 153.

Laund, *sb.* glade.

Lavolt, *sb.* a dance in which two persons bound high and
  whirl round.

Lay for, *v.t.* to strive to win.

Leasing, *sb.* lying, falsehood.

Leave, *sb.* liberty, license.

Leer, *sb.* complexion.

Leese, *v.t.* to lose.

Leet, *sb.* a manor court. T. of S. Ind. II. 87. The time when
  such is held. Oth. III. 3. 140.

Leiger, *sb.* ambassador.

Length, *sb.* delay.

Let, *v.t.* to hinder. Tw.N. V. 1. 246; Ham. I. 4. 85. Detain.
  W.T. I. 2. 41. Forbear. Lucr. 10. *p.p.* caused. Ham. IV. 6.
  11. *sb.* hindrance. H V. V. 2. 65.

Let-alone, *sb.* hindrance, prohibition.

Level, *sb.* aim, line of fire. R. & J. III. 3. 102. *v.i.* to aim. R
  III. IV. 4. 202. Be on the same level. Oth. I. 3. 239. *adv.*
  evenly. Tw.N. II. 4. 32.

Lewd, *adj.* base, vile.

Libbard, *sb.* leopard.

Liberal, *adj.* licentious. Liberal conceit = elaborate design. Ham. V. 2. 152. *adv.* freely, openly. Oth. V. 2. 220.

Lieger, *sb.* ambassador.

Lifter, *sb.* thief.

Light, *p.p.* lighted.

Likelihood, *sb.* sign, indication.

Lime, *v.t.* to put lime into liquor. M.W.W. I. 3. 14. Smear with bird-lime. 2 H VI. I. 3. 86. Catch with bird-lime. Tw.N. III. 4. 75. Cement. 3 H VI. V. 1. 84.

Limit, *sb.* appointed time. R II. I. 3. 151. *v.t.* to appoint. John. V. 2. 123.

Line, *v.t.* to draw, paint. As III. 2. 93. Strengthen, fortify. 1 H IV. II. 3. 85.

Line-grove, *sb.* a grove of lime trees.

Linsey-woolsey, *sb.* gibberish (literally, mixed stuff).

Lipsbury pinfold. Perhaps = between the teeth.

List, *sb.* desire, inclination. Oth. II. 1. 105. Limit, boundary. 1 H IV. IV. 1. 51. Lists for combat. Mac. III. 1. 70.

Lither, *adj.* flexible, gentle.

Livery, *sb.* delivery of a freehold into the possession of the heir.

Lob, *sb.* lubber, lout.

Lockram, *sb.* coarse linen.

Lodge, *v.t.* to lay flat, beat down.

Loggats, *sb.* a game somewhat resembling bowls.

Loof, *v.t.* to luff, bring close to the wind.

Losel, *sb.* a wasteful, worthless fellow.

Lout, *v.t.* to make a lout or fool of.

Lown, *sb.* base fellow.

Luce, *sb.* pike or jack.

Lurch, *v.t.* to win a love set at a game; bear off the prize easily. Cor. II. 2. 102. *v.i.* to skulk. M. W. W. II. 2. 25.

Lym, *sb.* bloodhound; so called from the leam or leash used to hold him.

Maggot-pie, *sb.* magpie.

Main, *sb.* a call at dice. 1 H IV. IV. 1. 47. Mainland. Lear, III. 1. 6. The chief power. Ham. V. 4. 15.

Main-course, *sb.* mainsail.

Main'd, *p.p.* maimed.

Makeless, *adj.* mateless, widowed.

Malkin, *sb.* slattern.

Mallard, *sb.* a wild drake.

Mallecho, *sb.* mischief (Span. *malhecho*).

Malt-horse, *sb.* brewer's horse.

Mammering, *pr.p.* hesitating.

Mammet, *sb.* a doll.

Mammock, *v.t.* to tear in pieces.

Manakin, *sb.* little man.

Mankind, *adj.* masculine, applied to a woman.

Manner, with the = in the act, red-handed.

Mare, *sb.* nightmare. To ride the wild mare = play at see-saw.

Mark, *sb.* thirteen shillings and fourpence.

Mart, *v.i.* to market, traffic. Cym. I. 6. 150. *v.t.* to vend, traffic with. J. C. IV. 3. 11.

Mastic, *sb.* used to stop decayed teeth.

Match, *sb.* compact, bargain. M. of V. III. 1. 40. Set a match = make an appointment. 1 H IV. 1. 2. 110.

Mate, *v.t.* to confound, make bewildered. C. of E. III. 2. 54. Match, cope with. H VIII. III. 2. 274.

Material, *adj.* full of matter.

Maugre, *prep.* in spite of.

Maund, *sb.* a basket.

Mazard, *sb.* skull.

Meacock, *adj.* spiritless, pusillanimous.

Mealed, *p.p.* mingled, compounded.

Mean, *sb.* the intermediate part between the tenor and treble.

Meiny, *sb.* attendants, retinue.

Mell, *v.i.* to meddle.

Mered, He being the mered question—the question concerning him alone. A. & C. III. 13. 10.

Mess, *sb*, a set of four. L.L.L. IV. 3. 204. Small quantity. 2 H IV. II. 1. 95. Lower messes = inferiors, as messing at the lower end of the table. W.T. I. 2. 226.

Mete, *v. i.* to mete at = aim at.

Metheglin, *sb.* a kind of mead, made of honey and water.

Micher, *sb.* truant.

Miching, *adj.* sneaking, stealthy.

Mineral, *sb.* a mine.

Minikin, *adj.* small, pretty.

Minion, *sb.* darling, favourite. John, II. 1. 392. Used contemptuously. 2 H VI. I. 3. 82. A pert, saucy person. 2 H VI. I. 3. 136.

Mirable, *adj.* admirable.

Mire, *v.i.* to be bemired, sink as into mire.

Misdread, *sb.* fear of evil.

Misprision, *sb.* mistake. M.N.D. III. 2. 90. Contempt. A.W. II. 3. 153.

Misproud, *adj.* viciously proud.

Miss, *sb.* misdoing.

Missingly, *adv.* regretfully.

Missive, *sb.* messenger.

Misthink, *v.t.* to misjudge.

Mobled, *p.p.* having the face or head muffled.

Modern, *adj.* commonplace, trite.

Module, *sb.* mould, form.

Moldwarp, *sb.* mole.

Mome, *sb.* blockhead, dolt.

Momentany, *adj.* momentary, lasting an instant.

Monster, *v.t.* to make monstrous.

Month's mind, *sb.* intense desire or yearning.

Moralize, *v.t.* to interpret, explain.

Mort, *sb.* trumpet notes blown at the death of the deer.

Mortal, *adj.* deadly.

Mortified, *p.p.* deadened, insensible.

Mot, *sb.* motto, device.

Mother, *sb.* the disease *hysterica passio*.

Motion, *v.t.* to propose, counsel. 1 H VI. I. 3. 63. *sb.* a puppet show. W.T. IV. 3. 96. A puppet. Two G. II. 1. 91. Solicitation, proposal, suit. C. of E. I. 1. 60. Emotion, feeling, impulse. Tw.N. II. 4. 18.

Motive, *sb.* a mover, instrument, member.

Mountant, *adj.* lifted up.

Mow, *sb.* a grimace. *v.i.* to grimace.

Moy, *sb.* probably some coin.

Muleter, *sb. muleteer.*

Mulled, *p.p.* flat, insipid.

Mummy, *sb.* a medical or magical preparation originally made from mummies.

Murdering-piece, *sb.* a cannon loaded with chain-shot.

Murrion, *adj.* infected with the murrain.

Muse, *v.i.* to wonder. John, III. 1. 317. *v.t.* to wonder at. Tp. III. 3. 36.

Muset, *sb.* a gap or opening in a hedge.

Muss, *sb.* scramble.

Mutine, *sb.* mutineer.

Mystery, *sb.* profession. M. for M. IV. 2. 28. Professional skill. A.W. III. 6. 65.

Nayword, *sb.* pass-word, M.W.W. II. 2. 126. A by-word. Tw.N. II. 3. 132.

Neat, *adj.* trim, spruce.

Neb, *sb.* bill or beak.

Neeld, *sb.* needle.

Neeze, *v.i.* to sneeze.

Neif, *sb.* fist.

Next, *adj.* nearest.

Nick, *sb.* out of all nick, beyond all reckoning.

Night-rule, *sb.* revelry.

Nill = will not.

Nine-men's-morris, *sb.* a rustic game.

Note, *sb.* list, catalogue. W.T. IV. 2. 47. Note of expectation = list of expected guests. Mac. III. 3. 10. Stigma, mark of reproach. R II. I. 1. 43. Distinction. Cym. II. 3. 12. knowledge, observation. Lear, III. 1. 18.

Nott-pated, *adj.* crop-headed.

Nousle, *v.t.* to nurse, nourish delicately.

Nowl, *sb.* noddle.

Nuthook, *sb.* slang for catchpole.

Oathable, *adj.* capable of taking an oath.

Object, *sb.* anything presented to the sight; everything that comes in the way.

Obsequious, *adj.* regardful of funeral rites. 3 H VI. II. 5. 118. Funereal, having to do with obsequies. T. A. V. 3. 153.

Observance, *sb.* observation. Oth. III. 3. 151. Homage. 2 H IV. IV. 3. 15. Ceremony. M. of V. II. 2. 194.

Obstacle, *sb.* blunder for obstinate.

Occupation, *sb.* trade (in contemptuous sense). Cor. IV. 1. 14. Voice of occupation = vote of working men. Cor. IV. 6. 98.

Odd, *adj.* unnoticed. Tp. I. 2. 223. At odds. T. & C. IV. 5. 265.

Oeillades, *sb.* amorous glances.

O' ergrown, *p.p.* bearded. Cym. IV. 4. 33. Become too old. M. for M. I. 3. 22.

O'erstrawed, *p.p.* overstrewn.

Office, *v.t.* to office all = do all the domestic service. A. W. III. 2. 128. Keep officiously. Cor. V. 2. 61.

Oneyers, *sb.* unexplained word.

Opposition, *sb.* combat, encounter.

Orb, *sb.* orbit. R. & J. II. 1. 151. Circle. M.N.D. II. 1. 9. A heavenly body. M. of V. V. 1. 60. The earth. Tw.N. III. 1. 39.

Ordinant, *adj.* ordaining, controlling.

Ordinary, *sb.* a public dinner at which each man pays for his own share.

Ort, *sb.* remnant, refuse.

Ouphs, *sb.* elves, goblins.

Outrage, *sb.* outburst of rage.

Overscutch'd, *p.p.* over-whipped, over-switched (perhaps in a wanton sense).

Overture, *sb.* disclosure. W.T. II. 1. 172. Declaration. Tw.N. I. 5. 208.

Owe, *v.t.* to own, possess.

Packing, *sb.* plotting, conspiracy.

Paddock, *sb.* toad. Ham. III. 4. 191. A familiar spirit in the form of a toad. Mac. I. 1. 9.

Pajock, *sb.* term of contempt, by some said to mean peacock.

Pale, *sb.* enclosure, confine.

Palliament, *sb.* robe.

Parcel-bawd, *sb.* half-bawd.

Paritor, *sb.* apparitor, an officer of the Bishops' Court.

Part, *sb.* party, side.

Partake, *v.t.* to make to partake, impart. W.T. V. 3. 132. To share. J.C. II. 1. 305.

Parted, *p.p.* endowed.

Partisan, *sb.* a kind of pike.

Pash, *sb.* a grotesque word for the head. W.T. I. 2. 128. *v.t.* to smite, dash. T. & C. II. 3. 202.

Pass, *v.t.* to pass sentence on. M. for M. II. 1. 19. Care for. 2 H VI. IV. 2. 127. Represent. L.L.L. V. 1. 123. Make a thrust in fencing. Tw.N. III. 1. 44.

Passage, *sb.* passing to and fro. C. of E. III. 1. 99. Departure, death. Ham. III. 3. 86. Passing away. 1 H VI. II. 5. 108. Occurrence. A.W. I. 1. 19. Process, course. R. & J. Prol. 9. Thy passages of life = the actions of thy life. 1 H IV. III. 2. 8. Passages of grossness = gross impositions. Tw.N. III. 2. 70. Motion. Cor. V. 6. 76.

Passant. In heraldry, the position of an animal walking.

Passion, *sb.* passionate poem. M.N.D. V. 1. 306; Sonn. XX. 2.

Passionate, *v.t.* to express with emotion. T.A. III. 2. 6. *adj.* displaying emotion. 2 H VI. I. 1. 104. Sorrowful. John, II. 1. 544.

Passy measures, a corruption of the Italian *passamezzo*, denoting a stately and measured step in dancing.

Patch, *sb.* fool.

Patchery, *sb.* knavery, trickery.

Patronage, *v.t.* to patronize, protect.

Pavin, *sb.* a stately dance of Spanish or Italian origin.

Pawn, *sb.* a pledge.

Peach, *v.t.* to impeach, accuse.

Peat, *sb.* pet, darling.

Pedascule, *sb.* vocative, pedant, schoolmaster.

Peevish, *adj.* childish, silly. 1 H VI. V. 3. 186. Fretful, wayward. M. of V. I. 1. 86.

Peise, *v.t.* to poise, balance. John, II. 1. 575. Retard by making heavy. M. of V. III. 2. 22. Weigh down. R III. V. 3. 106.

Pelt, *v.i.* to let fly with words of opprobrium.

Pelting, *adj.* paltry.

Penitent, *adj.* doing penance.

Periapt, *sb.* amulet.

Period, *sb.* end, conclusion. A. & C. IV. 2. 25. *v.t.* to put an end to. Tim. I. 1. 103.

Perked up, *p.p.* dressed up.

Perspective, *sb.* glasses so fashioned as to create an optical illusion.

Pert, *adj.* lively, brisk.

Pertaunt-like, *adv.* word unexplained and not yet satisfactorily amended. L.L.L. V. 2. 67.

Pervert, *v.t.* to avert, turn aside.

Pettitoes, *sb.* feet; properly pig's feet.

Pheeze, *v.t.* beat, chastise, torment.

Phisnomy, *sb.* physiognomy.

Phraseless, *adj.* indescribable.

Physical, *adj.* salutary, wholesome.

Pia mater, *sb.* membrane that covers the brain; used for the brain itself.

Pick, *v.t.* to pitch, throw.

Picked, *p.p.* refined, precise.

Picking, *adj.* trifling, small.

Piece, *sb.* a vessel of wine.

Pight, *p.p.* pitched.

Piled, *p.p* = peeled, bald, with quibble on 'piled' of velvet.

Pill, *v.t.* to pillage, plunder.

Pin, *sb.* bull's-eye of a target.

Pin-buttock, *sb.* a narrow buttock.

Pioned, *adj.* doubtful word: perhaps covered with marsh-marigold, or simply dug.

Pip, *sb.* a spot on cards. A pip out = intoxicated, with reference to a game called one and thirty.

Pitch, *sb.* the height to which a falcon soars, height.

Placket, *sb.* opening in a petticoat, or a petticoat.

Planched, *adj.* made of planks.

Plantage, *sb.* plants, vegetation.

Plantation, *sb.* colonizing.

Plausive, *adj.* persuasive, pleasing.

Pleached, *adj.* interlaced, folded.

Plurisy, *sb.* superabundance.

Point-devise, *adj.* precise, finical. L.L.L. V. 1.19. *adv.* Tw.N. II. 5. 162.

Poking-sticks, *sb.* irons for setting out ruffs.

Pole-clipt, *adj.* used of vineyards in which the vines are grown around poles.

Polled, *adj.* clipped, laid bare.

Pomander, *sb.* a ball of perfume.

Poor-John, *sb.* salted and dried hake.

Porpentine, *sb.* porcupine.

Portable, *adj.* supportable, endurable.

Portage, *sb.* port-hole. H V. III. 1. 10. Port-dues. Per. III. 1. 35.

Portance, *sb.* deportment, bearing.

Posse, *v.t.* to curdle.

Posy, *sb.* a motto on a ring.

Potch, *v.i.* to poke, thrust.

Pottle, *sb.* a tankard; strictly a two quart measure.

Pouncet-box, *sb.* a box for perfumes, pierced with holes.

Practice, *sb.* plot.

Practisant, *sb.* accomplice.

Practise, *v.i.* to plot, use stratagems. Two G. IV. 1. 47. *v.t.* to plot. John, IV. 1. 20.

Precedent, *sb.* rough draft. R III. III. 6. 7. Prognostic, indication. V. & A. 26.

Prefer, *v.t.* to promote, advance. Two G. II. 4. 154. Recommend. Cym. II. 3. 50. Present offer. M.N.D. IV. 2. 37.

Pregnant, *adj.* ready-witted, clever. Tw.N. II. 2. 28. Full of meaning. Ham. II. 2. 209. Ready. Ham. III. 2. 66. Plain, evident. M. for M. II. 1. 23.

Prenzie, *adj.* demure.

Pretence, *sb.* project, scheme.

Prick, *sb.* point on a dial. 3 H VI. I. 4. 34. Bull's-eye. L.L.L. IV. 1. 132. Prickle. As III. 2. 113. Skewer. Lear, II. 3. 16.

Pricket, *sb.* a buck of the second year.

Prick-song, *sb.* music sung from notes.

Prig, *sb.* a thief.

Private, *sb.* privacy. Tw.N. III. 4. 90. Private communication. John, IV. 3. 16.

Prize, *sb.* prize-contest. T.A. I. 1. 399. Privilege. 3 H VI. I. 4. 59. Value. Cym. III. 6. 76.

Probal, *adj.* probable, reasonable.

Proditor, *sb.* traitor.

Proface, *int.* much good may it do you!

Propagate, *v.t.* to augment.

Propagation, *sb.* augmentation.

Proper-false, *adj.* handsome and deceitful.

Property, *sb.* a tool or instrument. M.W.W. III. 4. 10. *v.t.* to make a tool of. John, V. 2. 79.

Pugging, *adj.* thievish.

Puisny, *adj.* unskilful, like a tyro.

Pun, *v.t.* to pound.

Punk, *sb.* strumpet.

Purchase, *v.t.* to acquire, get. *sb.* acquisition, booty.

Pursuivant, *sb.* a herald's attendant or messenger.

Pursy, *adj.* short-winded, asthmatic.

Puttock, *sb.* a kite.

Puzzel, *sb.* a filthy drab (Italian *puzzolente*).

Quaintly, *adv.* ingeniously, deliberately.

Qualification, *sb.* appeasement.

Quality, *sb.* profession, calling, especially that of an actor. Two G. IV. 1. 58. Professional skill. Tp. I. 2. 193.

Quarter, *sb.* station. John, V. 5. 20. Keep fair quarter = keep on good terms with, be true to. C. of E. II. 1. 108. In quarter = on good terms. Oth. II. 3. 176.

Quat, *sb.* pimple.

Quatch-buttock, *sb.* a squat or flat buttock.

Quean, *sb.* wench, hussy.

Queasiness, *sb.* nausea, disgust.

Queasy, *adj.* squeamish, fastidious. M.A. II. 1. 368. Disgusted. A. & C. III. 6. 20.

Quell, *sb.* murder.

Quest, *sb.* inquest, jury. R III. I. 4. 177. Search, inquiry, pursuit. M. of V. I. 1. 172. A body of searchers. Oth. I. 2. 46.

Questant, *sb.* aspirant, candidate.

Quicken, *v.t.* to make alive. A.W. II. 1. 76. Refresh, revive. M. of V. II. 7. 52. *v.i.* to become alive, revive. Lear, III. 7. 40.

Quietus, *sb.* settlement of an account.

Quill, *sb.* body. 2 H VI. I. 3. 3.

Quillet, *sb.* quibble.

Quintain, *sb.* a figure set up for tilting at.

Quire, *sb.* company.

Quittance, *v.i.* to requite. 1 H VI. II. 1. 14. *sb.* acquittance. M. W. W. I. 1. 10. Requital. 2 H IV. I. 1. 108.

Quoif, *sb.* cap.

Quoit, *v.t.* to throw.

Quote, *v.t.* to note, examine.

Rabato, *sb.* a kind of ruff.

Rabbit-sucker, *sb.* sucking rabbit.

Race, *sb.* root. W.T. IV. 3. 48. Nature, disposition. M. for M. II. 4. 160. Breed. Mac. II. 4. 15.

Rack, *v.t.* stretch, strain. M. of V. I. 1. 181. Strain to the utmost. *Cor.* V. 1. 16.

Rack, *sb.* a cloud or mass of clouds. Ham. II. 2. 492. *v.i.* move like vapour. 3 H VI. II. 1. 27.

Rampired, *p.p.* fortified by a rampart.

Ramps, *sb.* wanton wenches.

Ranges, *sb.* ranks.

Rap, *v.t.* to transport.

Rascal, *sb.* a deer out of condition.

Raught, *impf.* & *p.p.* reached.

Rayed, *p.p.* befouled. T. of S. IV. 1. 3. In T. of S. III. 2. 52 it perhaps means arrayed, *i.e.* attacked.

Raze, *sb.* root.

Razed, *p.p.* slashed.

Reave, *v.t.* to bereave.

Rebate, *v.t.* to make dull, blunt.

Recheat, *sb.* a set of notes sounded to call hounds off a false scent.

Rede, *sb.* counsel.

Reechy, *adj.* smoky, grimy.

Refell, *v.t.* to refute.

Refuse, *sb.* rejection, disowning. *v.t.* to reject, disown.

Reguerdon, *v.t.* to reward, guerdon.

Remonstrance, *sb.* demonstration.

Remotion, *sb.* removal.

Renege, *v.t.* to deny.

Renying, *pres. p.* denying.

Replication, *sb.* echo. J.C. I. 1. 50. Reply. Ham. IV. 2. 12.

Rere-mice, *sb.* bats.

Respected, blunder for suspected.

Respective, *adj.* worthy of regard. Two G. IV. 4. 197. Showing regard. John, I. 1. 188. Careful. M. of V. V. 1. 156.

Respectively, *adv.* respectfully.

Rest, *sb.* set up one's rest is to stand upon the cards in one's hand, be fully resolved.

Resty, *adj.* idle, lazy.

Resume, *v.t.* to take.

Reverb, *v.t.* to resound.

Revolt, *sb.* rebel.

Ribaudred, *adj.* ribald, lewd.

Rid, *v.t.* to destroy, do away with.

Riggish, *adj.* wanton.

Rigol, *sb.* a circle.

Rim, *sb.* midriff or abdomen.

Rivage, *sb.* shore.

Rival, *sb.* partner, companion. M.N.D. III. 2. 156. *v.i.* to be a competitor. Lear, I. I. 191.

Rivality, *sb.* partnership, participation.

Rivelled, *adj.* wrinkled.

Road, *sb.* roadstead, port. Two G. II. 4. 185. Journey. H VIII. IV. 2. 17. Inroad, incursion. H V. I. 2. 138.

Roisting, *adj.* roistering, blustering.

Romage, *sb.* bustle, turmoil.

Ronyon, *sb.* scurvy wretch.

Rook, *v.i.* to cower, squat.

Ropery, *sb.* roguery.

Rope-tricks, *sb.* knavish tricks.

Roping, *pr.p.* dripping.

Roted, *p.p.* learned by heart.

Rother, *sb.* an ox, or animal of the ox kind.

Round, *v.i.* to whisper. John, II. I. 566. *v.t.* to surround. M.N.D. IV. I. 52.

Round, *adj.* straightforward, blunt, plainspoken. C. of E. II. I. 82.

Rouse, *sb.* deep draught, bumper.

Rout, *sb.* crowd, mob. C. of E. III. I. 101. Brawl. Oth. II. 3. 210.

Row, *sb.* verse or stanza.

Roynish, *adj.* scurvy; hence coarse, rough.

Rub, *v.i.* to encounter obstacles. L.L.L. IV. I. 139. Rub on, of a bowl that surmounts the obstacle in its course. T. & C. III. 2. 49. *sb.* impediment, hindrance; from the game of bowls. John, III. 4. 128.

Ruffle, *v.i.* to swagger, bully. T.A. I. I. 314.

Ruddock, *sb.* the redbreast.

Rudesby, *sb.* a rude fellow.

Rump-fed, *adj.* pampered; perhaps fed on offal, or else fat-rumped.

Running banquet, a hasty refreshment (fig.).

Rush aside, *v.t.* to pass hastily by, thrust aside.

Rushling, blunder for rustling.

Sad, *adj.* grave, serious. M. of V. II. 2. 195. Gloomy, sullen. R II. V. 5. 70.

Sagittary, *sb.* a centaur. T. & C. V. 5. 14. The official residence in the arsenal at Venice. Oth. I. 1. 160.

Sallet, *sb.* a close-fitting helmet. 2 H VI. IV. 10. 11. A salad. 2 H VI. IV. 10. 8.

Salt, *sb.* salt-cellar. Two G. III. 1. 354. *adj.* lecherous. M. for M. V. 1. 399. Stinging, bitter. T. & C. I. 3. 371.

Salutation, *sb.* give salutation to my blood = make my blood rise.

Salute, *v.t.* to meet. John, II. 1. 590. To affect. H VIII. II. 3. 103.

Sanded, *adj.* sandy-coloured.

Say, *sb.* a kind of silk.

Scald, *adj.* scurvy, scabby. H V. V. 1. 5.

Scale, *v.t.* to put in the scales, weigh.

Scall = scald. M.W.W. III. 1. 115.

Scamble, *v.i.* to scramble.

Scamel, *sb.* perhaps a misprint for seamell, or seamew.

Scantling, *sb.* a scanted or small portion.

Scape, *sb.* freak, escapade.

Sconce, *sb.* a round fort. H V. III. 6. 73. Hence a protection for the head. C. of E. II. 2. 37. Hence the skull. Ham. V. 1. 106. *v.r.* to ensconce, hide. Ham. III. 4. 4.

Scotch, *sb.* notch. *v.t.* to cut, slash.

Scrowl, *v.i.* perhaps for to scrawl.

Scroyles, *sb.* scabs, scrofulous wretches.

Scrubbed, *adj.* undersized.

Scull, *sb.* shoal of fish.

Seal, *sb.* to give seals = confirm, carry out.

Seam, *sb.* grease, lard.

Seconds, *sb.* an inferior kind of flour.

Secure, *adj.* without care, confident.

Security, *sb.* carelessness, want of caution.

Seedness, *sb.* sowing with seed.

Seel, *v.t.* to close up a hawk's eyes.

Self-admission, *sb.* self-approbation.

Semblative, *adj.* resembling, like.

Sequestration, *sb.* separation.

Serpigo, *sb.* tetter or eruption on the skin.

Sessa, *int.* exclamation urging to speed.

Shard-borne, *adj.* borne through the air on shards.

Shards, *sb.* the wing cases of beetles. A. & C. III. 2. 20.
Potsherds. Ham. V. I. 254.

Sharked up, *p.p.* gathered indiscriminately.

Shealed, *p.p.* shelled.

Sheep-biter, *sb.* a malicious, niggardly fellow.

Shent, *p.p.* scolded, rebuked. M.W.W. I. 4. 36.

Shive, *sb.* slice.

Shog, *v.i.* to move, jog.

Shore, *sb.* a sewer.

Shrewd, *adj.* mischievous, bad.

Shrewdly, *adv.* badly.

Shrewdness, *sb.* mischievousness.

Shrieve, *sb.* sheriff.

Shrowd, *sb.* shelter, protection.

Siege, *sb.* seat. M. for M. IV. 2. 98. Rank. Ham IV. 7. 75.
Excrement. Tp. II. 2. III.

Significant, *sb.* sign, token.

Silly, *adj.* harmless, innocent. Two G. IV. I. 72. Plain,
simple. Tw.N. II. 4. 46.

Simular, *adj.* simulated, counterfeited. Cym. V. 5. 20. *sb.*
simulator, pretender. Lear, III. 2. 54.

Sitch, *adv.* and *conj.* since.

Skains-mates, *sb.* knavish companions.

Slab, *adj.* slabby, slimy.

Sleeve-hand, *sb.* wristband.

Sleided, *adj.* untwisted.

Slipper, *adj.* slippery.

Slobbery, *adj.* dirty.

145

Slubber, *v.t.* to slur over, do carelessly.

Smatch, *sb.* smack, taste.

Sneak-cup, *sb.* a fellow who shirks his liquor.

Sneap, *v.t.* to pinch, nip. L.L.L. I. I. 100. *sb.* snub, reprimand. 2 H IV. II. I. 125.

Sneck up, contemptuous expression = go and be hanged.

Snuff, *sb.* quarrel. Lear, III. I. 26. Smouldering wick of a candle. Cym. I. 6. 87. Object of contempt. A.W. I. 2. 60. Take in snuff = take offence at. L.L.L. V. 2. 22.

Sob, *sb.* a rest given to a horse to regain its wind.

Solidare, *sb.* a small coin.

Sonties, *sb.* corruption of saints.

Sooth, *sb.* flattery.

Soothers, *sb.* flatterers.

Sophy, *sb.* the Shah of Persia.

Sore, *sb.* a buck of the fourth year.

Sorel, *sb.* a buck of the third year.

Sort, *sb.* rank. M.A. I. I. 6. Set, company. R III. V. 3. 316. Manner. M. of V. I. 2. 105. Lot. T. & C. I. 3. 376.

Sort, *v.t.* to pick out. Two G. III. 2. 92. To rank. Ham. II. 2. 270. To arrange, dispose. R III. II. 2. 148. To adapt. 2 H VI. II. 4. 68. *v.i.* to associate. V. & A. 689. To be fitting. T. & C. I. I. 109. Fall out, happen. M.N.D. III. 2. 352.

Souse, *v.t.* to swoop down on, as a falcon.

Sowl, *v.t.* to lug, drag by the ears.

Span-counter, *sb.* boy's game of throwing a counter so as to strike, or rest within a span of, an opponent's counter.

Speed, *sb.* fortune, success.

Speken = speak.

Sperr, *v.t.* to bar.

Spital, *sb.* hospital.

Spital house, *sb.* hospital.

Spleen, *sb.* quick movement. M.N.D. I. I. 146. Fit of laughter. L.L.L. III. I. 76.

Spot, *sb.* pattern in embroidery.

Sprag, *adj.* sprack, quick, lively.

Spring, *sb.* a young shoot.

Springhalt, *sb.* a lameness in horses.

Spurs, *sb.* the side roots of a tree.

Squandering, *adj.* roving, random. As II. 7. 57.

Square, *sb.* the embroidery about the bosom of a smock or shift. W.T. IV. 3. 212. Most precious square of sense = the most sensitive part. Lear, I. 1. 74.

Square, *v.i.* to quarrel.

Squash, *sb.* an unripe peascod.

Squier, *sb.* square, rule.

Squiny, *v.i.* to look asquint.

Staggers, *sb.* giddiness, bewilderment. A.W. II. 3. 164. A disease of horses. T. of S. III. 2. 53.

Stale, *sb.* laughing stock, dupe. 3 H VI. III. 3. 260. Decoy. T. of S. III. 1. 90. Stalking-horse. C. of E. II. 1. 101. Prostitute. M.A. II. 2. 24. Horse-urine. A. & C. I. 4. 62.

Stamp, *v.t.* to mark as genuine, give currency to.

Standing, *sb.* duration, continuance. W.T. I. 2. 430. Attitude. Tim. I. 1. 34.

Standing-tuck, *sb.* a rapier standing on end.

Staniel, *sb.* a hawk, the kestrel.

Stare, *v.i.* to stand on end.

State, *sb.* attitude. L.L.L. IV. 3. 183. A chair of state. 1 H IV. II. 4. 390. Estate, fortune. M. of V. III. 2. 258. States (pl.) = persons of high position. John, II. 1. 395.

Statute-caps, *sb.* woollen caps worn by citizens as decreed by the Act of 1571.

Staves, *sb.* shafts of lances.

Stead, *v.t.* to help.

Stead up, *v.t.* to take the place of.

Stelled, *p.p.* fixed. Lucr. 1444. Sonn. XXIV. 1. Starry. Lear, III. 7. 62.

Stickler-like, *adj.* like a stickler, whose duty it was to separate combatants.

Stigmatic, *adj.* marked by deformity.

Stillitory, *sb.* a still.

Stint, *v.i.* to stop, cease. R. & J. I. 3. 48. *v.t.* to check, stop. T. & C. IV. 5. 93.

Stock, *sb.* a dowry. Two G. III. 1. 305. A stocking. Two G.
III. 1. 306; 1 H IV. II. 4. 118. A thrust in fencing.
M.W.W. II. 3. 24. *v.t.* to put in the stocks. Lear, II. 2.
333.

Stomach, *sb.* courage. 2 H IV. I. 1. 129. Pride. T. of S. V. 2.
177.

Stomaching, *sb.* resentment.

Stone-bow, *sb.* a cross-bow for shooting stones.

Stoop, *sb.* a drinking vessel.

Stricture, *sb.* strictness.

Stride, *v.t.* to overstep.

Stover, *sb.* cattle fodder.

Stuck, *sb.* a thrust in fencing.

Subject, *sb.* subjects, collectively.

Subscribe, *v.i.* to be surety. A.W. III. 6. 84. Yield, submit. 1
H VI. II. 4. 44. *v.t.* to admit, acknowledge. M.A. V. 2. 58.

Subtle, *adj.* deceptively smooth.

Successantly, *adv.* in succession.

Sufferance, *sb.* suffering. M. for M. II. 2. 167. Patience. M.
of V. I. 3. 109. Loss. Oth. II. 1. 23. Death penalty. H V.
II. 2. 158.

Suggest, *v.t.* to tempt.

Suit, *sb.* service, attendance. M. for M. IV. 4. 19. Out of
suits with fortune = out of fortune's service.

Supervise, *sb.* inspection.

Suppliance, *sb.* pastime.

Sur-addition, *sb.* an added title.

Surmount, *v.i.* to surpass, exceed. 1 H VI. V. 3. 191. *v.t.* to
surpass. L.L.L. V. 2. 677.

Sur-reined, *p.p.* overridden.

Suspect, *sb.* suspicion.

Swarth, *adj.* black. T.A. II. 3. 71. *sb.* swath. Tw.N. II. 3. 145.

Swoopstake, *adv.* in one sweep, wholesale.

Tag, *sb.* rabble.

Take, *v.t.* to captivate. W.T. IV. 3. 119. Strike. M.W.W. IV.
4. 32. Take refuge in. C. of E. V. 1. 36. Leap over. John,

V. 2. 138. Take in = conquer. A. & C. I. 1 .23. Take out = copy. Oth. III. 3. 296. Take thought = feel grief for. J.C. II. 1. 187. Take up = get on credit. 2 H VI. IV. 7. 125. Reconcile. Tw.N. III. 4. 294. Rebuke. Two G. I. 2. 134.

Tallow-keech, *sb.* a vessel filled with tallow.

Tanling, *sb.* one tanned by the sun. John, IV. 1. 117. Incite. Ham. II. 2. 358.

Tarre, *v.t.* to set on dogs to fight.

Taste, *sb.* trial, proof. *v.t.* to try, prove.

Tawdry-lace, *sb.* a rustic necklace.

Taxation, *sb.* satire, censure. As I. 2. 82. Claim, demand. Tw.N. I. 5. 210.

Teen, *sb.* grief.

Tenable, *adj.* capable of being kept.

Tend, *v.i.* to wait, attend. Ham. I. 3. 83. Be attentive. Tp. I. 1. 6. *v.t.* to tend to, regard. 2 H VI. I. 1. 204. Wait upon. A. & C. II. 2. 212.

Tendance, *sb.* attention. Tim. I. 1. 60. Persons attending. Tim. I. 1. 74.

Tender, *v.t.* to hold dear, regard. R III. I. 1. 44. *sb.* care, regard. 1 H IV. V. 4. 49.

Tender-hefted, *adj.* set in a delicate handle or frame.

Tent, *sb.* probe. T. & C. II. 2. 16. *v.t.* to probe. Ham. II. 2. 608. Cure. Cor. I. 9. 31.

Tercel, *sb.* male goshawk.

Termless, *adj.* not to be described.

Testerned, *p.p.* presented with sixpence.

Testril, *sb.* sixpence.

Tetchy, *adj.* irritable.

Tetter, *sb.* skin erruption. Ham. I. 5. 71. *v.t.* to infect with tetter. Cor. III. 1. 99.

Than = then, Lucr. 1440.

Tharborough, *sb.* third borough, constable.

Thick, *adv.* rapidly, close.

Thirdborough, *sb.* constable.

Thisne, perhaps = in this way. M.N.D. I. 2. 48.

Thoughten, *p.p.* be you thoughten = entertain the thought.

Thrall, *sb.* thraldom, slavery. Pass. P. 266. *adj.* enslaved. V. & A. 837.

Three-man beetle, a rammer operated by three men.

Three-man songmen, three-part glee-singers.

Three-pile, *sb.* the finest kind of velvet.

Three-piled, *adj.* having a thick pile. M. for M. I. 2. 32. Superfine (met.). L.L.L. V. 2. 407.

Tickle, *adj.* unstable. 2 H VI. I. 1. 216. Tickle of the sere, used of lungs readily prompted to laughter; literally hair-triggered. Ham. II. 2. 329.

Ticklish, *adj.* wanton.

Tight, *adj.* swift, deft. A. & C. IV. 4. 15. Water-tight, sound. T. of S. II. 1. 372.

Tightly, *adv.* briskly, smartly.

Time-pleaser, *sb.* time server, one who complies with the times.

Tire, *sb.* headdress. Two G. IV. 4. 187. Furniture. Per II. 2. 21.

Tire, *v.i.* to feed greedily. 3 H VI. I. 1. 269. *v.t.* make to feed greedily. Lucr. 417.

Tisick, *sb.* phthisic, a cough.

Toaze, *v.t.* to draw out, untangle.

Tod, *sb.* Twenty-eight pounds of wool. *v.t.* to yield a tod.

Toged, *adj.* wearing a toga.

Toll, *v.i.* to pay toll. A.W. V. 3. 147. *v.t.* to take toll. John, III. 1. 154.

Touch, *sb.* trait. As V. 4. 27. Dash, spice. R III. IV. 4. 157. Touchstone. R III. IV. 2. 8. Of noble touch = of tried nobility. Cor. IV. 1. 49. Brave touch = fine test of valour. M.N.D. III. 2. 70. Slight hint. H VIII. V. 1. 13. Know no touch = have no skill. R II. I. 3. 165.

Touse, *v.t.* to pull, tear.

Toy, *sb.* trifle, idle fancy, folly.

Tract, *sb.* track, trace. Tim. I. 1. 53. Course. H VIII. I. 1. 40.

Train, *v.t.* to allure, decoy. I H VI. I. 3. 25. *sb.* bait, allurement. Mac. IV. 3. 118.

Tranect, *sb.* ferry, a doubtful word.

Translate, *v.t.* to transform.

Trash, *v.t.* lop off branches. Tp. I. 2. 81. Restrain a dog by a trash or strap. Oth. II. 1. 307.

Traverse, *v.i.* to march to the right or left.

Tray-trip, *sb.* a game at dice, which was won by throwing a trey.

Treachors, *sb.* traitors.

Treatise, *sb.* discourse.

Trench, *v.t.* to cut. Two G. III. 2. 7. Divert from its course by digging. H IV. III. 1. 112.

Troll-my-dames, *sb.* the French game of *trou madame*, perhaps akin to bagatelle.

Tropically, *adv.* figuratively.

True-penny, *sb.* an honest fellow. Ham. I. 5. 150.

Try, *sb.* trial, test. Tim. VI. 1. 9. Bring to try = bring a ship as close to the wind as possible.

Tub, *sb.* and tubfast, *sb.* a cure of venereal disease by sweating and fasting.

Tuck, *sb.* rapier.

Tun-dish, *sb.* funnel.

Turk, to turn Turk = to be a renegade. M.A. III. 4. 52. Turk Gregory = Pope Gregory VII. 1 H IV. V. 3. 125.

Twiggen, *adj.* made of twigs or wicker.

Twilled, *adj.* perhaps, covered with sedge or reeds.

Twire, *v.i.* to twinkle.

Umber, *sb.* a brown colour.

Umbered, *p.p.* made brown, darkened.

Umbrage, *sb.* a shadow.

Unaneled, *adj.* not having received extreme unction.

Unbarbed, *adj.* wearing no armour, bare.

Unbated, *adj.* unblunted.

Unbraced, *adj.* unbuttoned.

Uncape, *v.i.* to uncouple, throw off the hounds.

Uncase, *v.i.* to undress.

Unclew, *v.t.* to unwind, undo.

Uncolted, *p.p.* deprived of one's horse. 1 H IV. II. 2. 41.

Uncomprehensive, *adj.* incomprehensible.

Unconfirmed, *adj.* inexperienced.

Undercrest, *v.t.* to wear upon the crest.

Undertaker, *sb.* agent, person responsible to another for something.

Underwrite, *v.t.* to submit to.

Undistinguished, *adj.* not to be seen distinctly, unknowable.

Uneath, *adv.* hardly, with difficulty.

Unfolding, *adj.* unfolding star, the star at whose rising the shepherd lets the sheep out of the fold.

Unhappy, *adj.* mischievous, unlucky.

Unhatched, *p.p.* unhacked. Tw.N. III. 4. 234. Undisclosed. Oth. III. 4. 140.

Unhouseled, *adj.* without having received the sacrament.

Union, *sb.* large pearl.

Unkind, *adj.* unnatural. Lear, I. 1. 261. Childless. V. & A. 204.

Unlived, *p.p.* deprived of life.

Unpaved, *adj.* without stones.

Unpinked, *adj.* not pinked, or pierced with eyelet holes.

Unraked, *adj.* not made up for the night.

Unrecuring, *adj.* incurable.

Unrolled, *p.p.* struck off the roll.

Unseeming, *pr.p.* not seeming.

Unseminared, *p.p.* deprived of seed or virility.

Unset, *adj.* unplanted.

Unshunned, *adj.* inevitable.

Unsifted, *adj.* untried, inexperienced.

Unsquared, *adj.* unsuitable.

Unstate, *v.t.* to deprive of dignity.

Untented, *adj.* incurable.

Unthrift, *sb.* prodigal. *adj.* good for nothing.

Untraded, *adj.* unhackneyed.

Unyoke, *v.t.* to put off the yoke, take ease after labour. Ham. V. 1. 55. *v.t.* to disjoin. John, III. 1. 241.

Up-cast, *sb.* a throw at bowls; perhaps the final throw.

Upshoot, *sb.* decisive shot.

Upspring, *sb.* a bacchanalian dance.

Upstaring, *adj.* standing on end.

Urchin, *sb.* hedgehog. T.A. II. 3. 101. A goblin. M.W.W. IV. 4. 49.

Usance, *sb.* interest.

Use, *sb.* interest. M.A. II. 1. 269. Usage. M. for M. I. 1. 40. In use = in trust. M. of V. IV. 1. 383.

Use, *v.r.* to behave oneself.

Uses, *sb.* manners, usages.

Utis, *sb.* boisterous merriment.

Vade, *v.i.* to fade.

Vail, *sb.* setting (of the sun). T. & C. V. 8. 7. *v.t.* to lower, let fall. 1 H VI. V. 3. 25. *v.i.* to bow. Per. IV. Prol. 29.

Vails, *sb.* a servant's perquisites.

Vain, for vain = to no purpose.

Vantbrace, *sb.* armour for the forearm.

Vast, *adj.* waste, desolate, boundless.

Vaunt-couriers, *sb.* fore-runners.

Vaward, *sb.* vanguard. 1 H VI. I. 1. 132. The first part. M.N.D. IV. 1. 106.

Vegetives, *sb.* plants.

Velvet-guards, *sb.* velvet linings, used metaphorically of those who wear them. 1 H IV. III. 1. 256.

Veney, or venew, *sb.* a fencing bout, a hit.

Venge, *v.t.* to avenge.

Vent, *sb.* discharge. Full of vent = effervescent like wine.

Via, *interj.* away, on!

Vice, *sb.* the buffoon in old morality plays. R III. III. 1. 82. *v.t.* to screw (met.) W.T. I. 2. 415.

Vinewedst, *adj.* mouldy, musty.

Violent, *v.i.* to act violently, rage.

Virginalling, *pr.p.* playing with the fingers as upon the virginals.

Virtuous, *adj.* efficacious, powerful. Oth. III. 4 .110. Essential. M.N.D. III. 2. 367. Virtuous season = benignant influence. M. for M. II. 2. 168.

Vouch, *sb.* testimony, guarantee. 1 H VI. V. 3. 71. *v.i.* to assert, warrant.

Vizard, *sb.* mask.

Waft, *v.t.* to beckon. C. of E. II. 2. 108. To turn. W.T. I. 2. 371.

Wag, *v.i.* and *v.t.* to move, stir. R III. III. 5. 7. To go one's way. M.A. V. 1. 16.

Wage, *v.t.* to stake, risk. 1 H IV. 4. 20. *v.i.* to contend. Lear, II. 4. 210. Wage equal = be on an equality with. A. & C. v. 1. 31.

Wanion, *sb.* with a wanion = with a vengeance.

Wanton, *sb.* one brought up in luxury, an effeminate person. John, V. 1. 70. *v.i.* to dally, play. W.T. II. 1. 18.

Wappened, *p.p.* of doubtful meaning, perhaps worn out, stale.

Ward, *sb.* guardianship. A.W. I. 1. 5. Defence. L.L.L. III. 1. 131. Guard in fencing. 1 H IV. II. 4. 198. Prison, custody. 2 H VI. V. 1. 112. Lock, bolt. Tim. III. 3. 38. *v.t.* to guard. R III. V. 3. 254.

Warden-pies, *sb.* pies made with the warden, a large baking pear.

Warrantize, *sb.* security, warranty.

Warrener, *sb.* keeper of a warren, gamekeeper.

Watch, *sb.* a watch candle that marked the hours.

Watch, *v.t.* to tame by keeping from sleep.

Waters, *sb.* for all waters = ready for anything.

Wealsmen, *sb.* statesmen.

Web and pin. *sb.* cataract of the eye.

Weeding, *sb.* weeds.

Weet, *v.t.* to know.

Welkin, *sb.* the blue, the sky. Tw.N. II. 3. 61. *adj.* sky-blue. W.T. I. 2. 136.

Whiffler, *sb.* one who cleared the way for a procession, carrying the whiffle or staff of his office.

Whist, *adj.* still, hushed.

Whittle, *sb.* a clasp-knife.

Whoobub, *sb.* hubbub.

Widowhood, *sb.* rights as a widow.

Wilderness, *sb.* wildness.

Wimpled, *p.p.* blindfolded. (A wimple was a wrap or handkerchief for the neck.)

Winchester goose, *sb.* a venereal swelling in the groin, the brothels of Southwark being in the jurisdiction of the Bishop of Winchester.

Window-bars, *sb.* lattice-like embroidery worn by women across the breast.

Windring, *adj.* winding.

Wink, *sb.* a closing of the eyes, sleep. Tp. II. I. 281. *v.i.* to close the eyes, be blind, be in the dark. C. of E. III. 2. 58.

Winter-ground, *v.t.* to protect a plant from frost by bedding it with straw.

Wipe, *sb.* a brand, mark of shame.

Wise-woman, *sb.* a witch.

Witch, *sb.* used of a man also; wizard.

Woman, *v.t.* woman me = make me show my woman's feelings.

Woman-tired, *adj.* henpecked.

Wondered, *p.p.* performing wonders.

Wood, *adj.* mad.

Woodman, *sb.* forester, hunter. M.W.W. V. 5. 27. In a bad sense, a wencher. M. for M. IV. 4. 163.

Woollen, to lie in the = either to lie in the blankets, or to be buried in flannel, as the law in Shakespeare's time prescribed.

Word, *sb.* to be at a word = to be as good as one's word.

Word, *v.t.* to represent. Cym. I. 4. 15. To deceive with words. A. & C. V. 2. 191.

World, *sb.* to go to the world = to be married. A woman of the world = a married woman. A world to see = a marvel to behold.

Wrangler, *sb.* an opponent, a tennis term.

Wreak, *sb.* revenge. T.A. IV. 3. 33. *v.t.* to revenge. T.A. IV. 3. 51.

Wreakful, *adj.* revengeful.

Wrest, *sb.* a tuning-key.

Wring, *v.i.* to writhe.

Write, *v.r.* to describe oneself, claim to be. Writ as little beard = claimed as little beard. A.W. II. 3. 62.

Writhled, *adj.* shrivelled up, wrinkled.

Wry, *v.i.* to swerve.

Yare, *adj.* and *adv.* ready, active, nimble.

Yarely, *adv.* readily, briskly.

Yearn, *v.t.* and *v.i.* to grieve.

Yellows, *sb.* jaundice in horses.

Yerk, *v.t.* to lash out at, strike quickly.

Yest, *sb.* froth, foam.

Yesty, *adj.* foamy, frothy.

Younker, *sb.* a stripling, youngster novice.

Yslaked, *p.p.* brought to rest.

Zany, *sb.* a fool, buffoon.

BIBLIOGRAPHY

Ackroyd, Peter, *Shakespeare: The Biography*, Vintage, 2006

Bloom, Harold, *William Shakespeare's 'As You Like It'*, Chelsea House, 1991

Greg, Walter Wilson, *Lodge's 'Rosalynde' Being the Original of Shakespeare's 'As You Like It'*, BiblioBazaar, 2009

Halliday, F.E., *A Shakespeare Companion*, Penguin, 1964

Holden, Anthony, *William Shakespeare: An Illustrated Biography*, Little, Brown, 2002

Hunt, Maurice A., *Shakespeare's As You Like It: Late Elizabethan Culture and Literary Representation*, Palgrave Macmillan, 2008

Rowse, A.L., *William Shakespeare: A Biography*, HarperCollins, 1963

Sowerby, Robin, *York Notes on William Shakespeare's 'As You Like It'*, Longman, 1999